Contents

The Department of National Heritage

Library Information Series No. 22

Investing in Children
The Future of Library Services for Children and Young People

Library and Information Services Council (England)

Working Party on Library Services for Children and Young People

LONDON: HMSO

ISBN 0 11 701994 1 ✓

The Department of National Heritage
2–4 Cockspur Street
London
SW1Y 5DH
Switchboard: 071–211 6000

Foreword by the Secretary of State

I am delighted that my library advisory body, the Library and Information Services Council (England), initiated this extensive review of the library and information needs of children and young people and of the extent to which those needs are being met by existing library services.

Our libraries are no longer concerned solely with books, but try to meet the literary needs of children, and their desire for information, in a variety of media from CD Rom to posters and prints. However, the fundamental need is still for children to learn to read, and research has shown that key factors in helping them do so successfully are, on the one hand, being read to, and, on the other, access to, and the availability of a wide range of books and stories. In making available this wide range of material, the potential of the library as a force in encouraging reading and information literacy cannot be too strongly emphasised. This report, therefore, takes as its starting point and overriding concern the needs of the child for books *per se* and the library services that provide them.

Library and information services for children and young people are provided in a variety of ways and through a variety of agencies, including public libraries, schools library services and libraries in schools. The emphasis placed by 'Investing in Children' on the need for all the relevant agencies within a given local authority area to develop an integrated strategy for delivering library services to children and young people is welcome. It will allow resources to be used to the best effect and help to ensure that children and young people have equality of access to library facilities and services, with a proper priority accorded to their needs. I commend this report to councillors and senior service managers in education and library authorities.

STEPHEN DORRELL
Secretary of State

Open letter to the Secretary of State for National Heritage

The membership of the Working Party responsible for producing the 'Investing in Children' report on LISC (England)'s behalf reflected a broad range of consumer and provider interests. The terms of reference agreed at its first meeting included a declared intention to "examine the way in which library services for children and young people are provided through the public library service, school and further education libraries, and the schools library service".

In the event, it became evident that within the resources and time-scale available, the Working Party could not consider the whole range of library services provided for children and young people in all possible age groups. Within an overriding concern with the needs of the child for books *per se* and the library services that provide for them, the Working Party's primary focus was therefore agreed to be on public library services for children and young people in the age group 0 to 16 years of age.

School library provision for children and young people was considered in our earlier report 'School libraries: the foundations of the curriculum', the recommendations of which have been revisited during the deliberations of this Working Party and the majority of which have been found to be still valid in broad terms.

It was apparent from the submissions made to the Working Party, however, that there are important issues around the provision of library services to young people in further education which need urgently to be pursued, and to which the Working Party was unable to do justice. LISC (England) therefore believes most strongly that work should be put speedily in hand to investigate library provision in the further education sector, using the same consumer-focused approach adopted in 'Investing in Children'. As Chairman, I urge you and your colleague the Secretary of State for Education to pursue this proposal at an early date.

SIR PETER SWINNERTON-DYER
Chairman, LISC (England)

Executive summary: key conclusions and recommendations

The Working Party has reached the following key conclusions, which form the foundation from which our recommendations arise.

- The role, function and mission of library services for children and young people have to be seen in the round, with integration of the major channels of delivery – the public library service for children and young people, the schools library service, and libraries in individual schools – at strategic level.

- The potential of the public library as a force in support of reading and information literacy cannot be too strongly emphasised.

- Problems in public and education library services for children and young people are evident in:
    - inequality of access to facilities and services;
    - wide disparities in standards of provision across the country;
    - lack of integration of services;
    - failure to accord proper priority to children and their needs;
    - inadequate or no research into reading and information needs.

- The way forward lies in:
    - identification and dissemination of innovative practice;
    - implementation of our recommendations;
    - a continuing base of research and statistical information.

The recommendations that follow have been agreed by the Working Party as pragmatic steps towards preventing what we see as present problems from cumulating into a future crisis. They flow from the general to the specific and are addressed to a wide range of bodies and officials, as follows:

Audience	Recommendations
Department of National Heritage (DNH)★	1,2,3,7,9,11,12,16,17
Department for Education (DFE)	1,17,19
Office for Standards in Education (OFSTED)	1,10,19,21
Training and Enterprise Councils (TECs)	1
Audit Commission	11
Chief Executives/Local Authorities	6,8,13,15
Library Managers	2,4,5,7,8,9,13,14,15,20
School Governing Bodies and Head Teachers	6,19,20
British Library (BL)	16
Library Association (LA)	7,9,10,16
Federation of Local Authority Chief Librarians (FOLACL)	16,18
Library and Information Statistics Unit (LISU)	9,10
CIPFA Statistical Information Service	10

School Curriculum Assessment Authority (SCAA)	17
Book Trust	10
Educational Publishers' Council (EPC)	10
Research Bodies	16

*Recommendations addressed to the Department of National Heritage in respect of public libraries in England imply mediation through the Welsh Office where they apply equally to public libraries in Wales.

These are the Working Party's Recommendations:

■ Recommendation 1

Each local authority should publish an integrated strategy for delivering library and information services to meet the identified needs of children and young people throughout its area, taking into account the roles, relationships and responsibilities of the major elements in the service – the public library, the schools library service, and libraries in individual schools – and involving other agencies as appropriate, eg, further education colleges, Training and Enterprise Councils. [S.5.2]

The strategy should take due account of recognised standards relating to services for children and young people. [S.5.3.3]

Inspection and monitoring should form a part of the strategy. [S.4.1.3, 4.2.3, 5.2]

– Chief Executives of authorities with education and library functions; DNH; DFE; OFSTED; TECs

■ Recommendation 2

The satisfaction of children's and young people's needs as individuals should be recognised and promoted as a core element of the public library service, central to its role in the promotion of literacy and its role in relation to educational institutions as defined in Recommendation 1. [S.4.1.1, 5.3]

– DNH (Review of the Public Library Service); Library Managers

■ Recommendation 3

The proposed Library and Information Commission should advise Government regarding its national role in support of libraries and information services and literacy programmes for children and young people. [S.5.2]

– DNH (Library and Information Commission)

■ Recommendation 4

There must be clear objectives for services to children and young people, and clear priorities should be established for children's needs across ages and stages of development. The objectives should accommodate the promotion of services to the child population as an integral and vital part of service provision, and should acknowledge the duty of public libraries to work with parents and carers of young children. [S.2, 5.3.2, 5.6.3, 5.6.5]

– Library Managers

■ **Recommendation 5**

The public library has a duty to meet children's need and desire for information in a range of media as well as books. It should provide information in appropriate media and formats, and whatever technology is needed to deliver them, and should promote their availability and use. [S.5.6.9]

- Library Managers

■ **Recommendation 6**

A multi-service Charter for the Child, drawn up jointly by all departments of the local authority that provide services for children, and published by the local authority, should set out the child's entitlement to service in general, including what he or she can reasonably expect from library services as defined in the integrated strategy proposed in Recommendation 1. The charter should be reviewed regularly for the relevance and currency of its content, and its impact should be monitored. [S.5.6.10]

- Local Authorities; School Governing Bodies

■ **Recommendation 7**

The Department of National Heritage should initiate work on a model charter which can be adapted for local use and published by public libraries as a Charter for the Reader relating to children and their needs. Such a charter might include the responsibilities of the organisation to ensure that staff are adequately trained, to provide accessible service and customer care in relation to children, and to properly investigate the needs of children and their parents and carers, recognising the differing needs of different age groups, cultures, backgrounds and stages of development. [S.5.3.1]

- DNH; Library Managers; LA

■ **Recommendation 8**

The percentage of the total materials budget applied to services for children and young people should be determined locally and should be at least the same as the percentage of children and young people in the population served. [S.4.1.2]

- Library Authorities; Library Managers

■ **Recommendation 9**

There should be model standards for services for children and young people, specifying minimum levels of provision and entitlement. In order to facilitate their acceptance by local authorities, they should be drawn up by the Library Association, with its specialist groups, in consultation with the local authority associations and the Department of National Heritage. They should be accepted and adapted by local authorities as part of their statutory responsibility to provide services for children through public libraries. Their application should be monitored by DNH as part of its overall monitoring responsibilities. [S.5.3.3]

- LA; Library Managers; DNH; LISU

■ **Recommendation 10**

Adequate statistical information should be produced, and trends monitored, to establish a comprehensive national picture of services and levels of provision, and to identify disparities in standards of service in order to facilitate local decision making. [S.4.4]

Co-ordination of data gathering between agencies that already collect data on library services and book provision for children should be investigated, and effected if feasible. [S.4.4]

– LISU; CIPFA; OFSTED; LA and its specialist groups; Book Trust; EPC

■ Recommendation 11

The Department of National Heritage should take the lead in the development of national performance indicators which reflect the rights and entitlements of children, and include at least a basic indicator for a child's rights to reading materials and library services. [S.5.3.4]

A model set of performance indicators specific to children's services, which will measure performance against defined objectives, taking into account quality aspects that are important to the user, should be developed for local use where indicators are not already in place in the local authority. [S.5.3.4]

– DNH; Audit Commission

■ Recommendation 12

The role of the Department of National Heritage in monitoring the whole public library service, and assessment procedures specified by it for this purpose, should include explicit reference to services for children and young people. [S.4.1.3]

– DNH

■ Recommendation 13

Every library authority should have a strategy to ensure and promote equal access to its resources for children and young people. [S.4.1.4]

– Library Authorities; Library Managers

■ Recommendation 14

The public library's senior management team (or equivalent) should include a person with designated overall responsibility for services to children and young people. [S.4.1.5]

– Library Managers

■ Recommendation 15

Every library authority should have a strategy for specialist training of staff engaged in work with children and young people. [S.4.1.6]

– Library Authorities; Library Managers

■ Recommendation 16

Priority should be given to research which explores the benefits, impacts and effectiveness of library provision for children and young people. [S.3.5]

There should be further investigation into how research and data relating to children's and young people's reading and library needs can be most effectively disseminated nationally. A national body such as the Library Association, with its specialist groups, should investigate the feasibility of an annual digest of information. [S.2.1, 2.2]

– BL; DNH (Library and Information Commission); Research Bodies; FOLACL Public Library Research Group; LA

■ **Recommendation 17**

The Department for Education and the Department of National Heritage, together with other relevant bodies such as the School Curriculum Assessment Authority, should initiate and co-ordinate work on issues relating to library book provision to support children's learning. DNH should take the lead in this work. [S.4.2.3]

– DFE; DNH; SCAA

■ **Recommendation 18**

When the Federation of Local Authority Chief Librarians (FOLACL) supersedes its present constituent organisations in 1996 as a single representative body for chief librarians, the opportunity should be taken to merge the existing specialist groups, AMDECL, SOCCEL, and YELL, into a similar single forum. [S.3.5]

– FOLACL

■ **Recommendation 19**

The Department for Education should issue guidance which reflects the need for support through books, learning resources and specialist advice, to enable schools to deliver the National Curriculum. DFE should ask OFSTED and school governing bodies to monitor local provision against this guidance. [S.4.2.2]

DFE is also asked to note the 1984 LISC Report *School libraries: the foundations of the curriculum*, and to continue to support its Recommendations 13.2.1/3/5/7 and 13.4.1, which remain valid despite the changes which have occurred in the organisation and management of schools. [S.5.4]

– DFE; OFSTED; School Governing Bodies and Head Teachers

■ **Recommendation 20**

School governing bodies should have a strategy for meeting the library and information needs of the curriculum, as part of the school's curriculum policy, and should keep this under review through a mechanism such as an annual report or review. [S.4.2.3, 5.4]

The strategy should promote teachers' knowledge of children's literature and understanding of information skills, and ensure that there are means through which this can be achieved. There should be co-ordination between librarians and teachers, and INSET for teachers should draw on the specialist skills of librarians in the public library's children's service and the schools library service, as happens already in some schools. [S.4.2.4]

Schools should introduce children to the public library service. [S.4.2.4]

– School Governing Bodies and Head Teachers; Library Managers

■ **Recommendation 21**

The criteria contained in the OFSTED *Handbook* for use in inspections to judge the adequacy of library provision and use should be expanded, sharpened and made more explicit, possibly through the inclusion of a Technical Paper on inspecting libraries in the *Handbook*. [S.4.2.3, 5.4]

– OFSTED

Acronyms used in the text

ACRE	Action with Communities in Rural England
ALCL	Association of London Chief Librarians
AMDCL	Association of Metropolitan District Chief Librarians
AMDECL	Association of Metropolitan District Education and Children's Librarians
AVC	Audiovisual and computer materials
BL	The British Library
BLR&DD	The British Library Research and Development Department
CBF	Children's Book Foundation (now Young Book Trust)
CCT	Compulsory Competitive Tendering
CIPFA	Chartered Institute of Public Finance and Accountancy
COSLA	Convention of Scottish Local Authorities
DFE	Department for Education (formerly DES, Department of Education and Science)
DNH	Department of National Heritage (which in April 1992 subsumed the former Office of Arts and Libraries (OAL)
ELG	Education Librarians Group (of the Library Association)
EPC	Educational Publishers Council
ERA	Education Reform Act
FOLACL	Federation of Local Authority Chief Librarians
GCSE	General Certificate of Secondary Education
GEST	Grants for Education Support and Training
GM	Grant-Maintained (Schools)
HMI	Her Majesty's Inspectorate
INSET	In-service training
LA	Library Association
LIS	Librarianship and Information Studies (Schools/Departments)
LISC	Library and Information Services Council (England); there are equivalent LISCs for Wales and Northern Ireland; in Scotland the equivalent is the Scottish Library and Information Council, SLIC
LISU	Library and Information Statistics Unit, Loughborough University of Technology
LMS	Local Management of Schools
NC	National Curriculum
OFSTED	Office for Standards in Education
OPAC	Online Public Access Catalogue
PLDIS	Public Library Development Incentive Scheme
SCAA	School Curriculum Assessment Authority
SCL	Society of County Librarians
SLA	School Library Association
SLG	School Libraries Group (of the Library Association)
SLS	Schools Library Services
SOCCEL	Society of County Children's and Education Librarians
TEC	Training and Enterprise Council
YELL	Youth and Education Librarians London
YLG	Youth Libraries Group (of the Library Association)

1 Background and scope of the review

1.1 Origin of the review

In 1984, the influential Library and Information Services Council (LISC) report *School libraries: the foundations of the curriculum* was published, carrying its message of the importance of school libraries and schools library services in teaching children to learn.[1] This stirred within the library profession calls for a similar exercise to be carried out for children's services in public libraries, leading to a submission to LISC in 1987 from the Society of County Children's and Education Librarians and the Association of Metropolitan District Education and Children's Librarians, with the support of the Society of County Librarians and the Association of Metropolitan District Chief Librarians, expressing concern over the state of library services for children and young people and urging that LISC should undertake an "objective re-appraisal of public library services to children".

The proposal was not immediately taken up, although LISC's interest in the whole area continued, particularly in school libraries in the context of the Government's proposals for education reform. In October 1991, at the launch by the Minister for the Arts of the Library Association's newly-published guidelines for public library services for children and young people, the question of the need for a special investigation and report was referred back to LISC.[2]

At its meeting on 7 November 1991, LISC agreed that a working group, under the chairmanship of David Leabeater of the National Consumer Council, "should be set up to invite evidence from interested groups against set terms of reference. These would cover the inter-relationships between libraries within schools, the school library service, and the service within the public library service".

1.2 Composition of the Working Party

The composition of the Working Party is given in Appendix A.

All countries of the UK were invited to join the Working Party. Scotland declined, and has not been represented. Northern Ireland accepted, and LISC (Northern Ireland) has had an observer throughout. LISC (Wales) initially had an observer, but its subsequent request for full participation was granted in August 1993 and it was represented at meetings from October 1993.

Apart from the professional interest groups involved in the subject area, numerous in themselves, there was a very wide range of organisations which might be interested in representation on the Working Party. The membership as finally determined reflected a broad range of consumer and provider interests. However, it was concluded that the interests of many organisations could best be served through their submission of evidence at an appropriate point rather than their representation over a long period of time. Organisations invited to submit evidence are listed in Appendix B.

1.3 Terms of reference

The terms of reference, as agreed at the first meeting of the Working Party, were to:

(i) **examine the library needs of children and young people and the extent to which they are being met by existing services and levels of staffing;**

(ii) **examine the way in which library services for children and young people are provided through the public library service, school and further education libraries, and the schools library service;**

(iii) **review recent research and development work into library services for children and young people, and assess its effectiveness and impact on services;**

(iv) **examine the effect of external change on the library needs of children and young people and on library services for them;**

(v) **recommend improvements, and how to bring them about, in library services for children and young people.**

1.4 Definitions: users and providers

In considering these terms of reference, it became evident that, given the resources and time-scale at its disposal, the Working Party could not consider the whole range of library services available to children and young people in all possible age groups.

We eventually became convinced that our overriding concern should be with the needs of the child for books *per se* and with the library services that provide for them. Within this overriding concern, the Working Party's primary focus was agreed as being on:

● children and young people in the age group 0 to 16;

● services for them provided by public libraries.

The age range to be considered was not defined in the terms of reference. There is in fact no standard definition of 'children and young people': the starting point is normally accepted as age 0 but the upper limit varies between 16 (normally the end of the school years) 19 (the end of the teenage years) and 26 (taken as the upper limit by the National Children's Bureau and promoted by at least one London borough).

In public libraries, the age of transfer from children's to adult services indicates the age range to which children's services are targeted. Statistics compiled by the Library and Information Statistics Unit (LISU) for 1992/93 show that while 76 public library authorities cite 14 as the age of transfer, there is considerable variation between the lowest age of transfer (11) and the highest (18). "In practice authorities do not rigidly define this transfer from children's to adult services; in some libraries there is a separate category for teenagers, while in others the age of transfer is at the discretion of parents or the librarian."[3]

In the end, the definition adopted was conditioned by the need to maintain a manageable remit. Within the age range considered, children and young people have been taken to include those of minority ethnic origins, those with disabilities, and others whose needs may be regarded as being in some way special.

Children and young people do not form a homogeneous group. Their need for books, and for libraries providing books and other material and services, is defined by ages and by stages of development, and changes rapidly over relatively short periods of time. Within the range 0 to 16, there are numerous different target audiences, such as pre-school children and teenagers.

For children in the pre-school age group (roughly 0 to 5) the public library provides the only library service to which they are entitled by right, and consideration of their needs must take into account the needs of their parents and carers also. For children in the school years, there is a need for an integrated approach between libraries in local authority and education sectors to support the needs arising from the National Curriculum, and broader educational needs, and also to fulfil leisure and recreational needs.

In agreeing our focus on public library services for children and young people, we were aware that the provision of books to children and young people involves not only public libraries, but also:

- schools library services;

- school libraries;

- libraries provided by agencies other than local authorities.

And that in considering the inter-relationships between all these, other sectors could be looked at even though resources could not be devoted to their full investigation.

The Working Party deliberated at length as to the feasibility of including further education within its remit. College libraries form only a small element in the network of channels through which library services are delivered to young people, and in the context of the definitions set out above, could only be a marginal issue for this review. In part, this decision was certainly influenced by the lack of comprehensive and current data on libraries in further education and of properly-researched information on the needs of students in this sector.

It has been made very clear to us, both by members of our own Working Party and by professional bodies submitting evidence, that **the whole area of library and learning resource provision in the further education sector subsequent to the 1992 Further and Higher Education Act requires in–depth investigation to ascertain the existing situation with regard to the provision of resources and the needs of students, and the ways in which development should take place.**

1.5   Service initiatives

The ways in which libraries are meeting needs, and the ways in which they might meet them in the future, are illustrated in the following pages by references to service initiatives, set out in boxes within the text. Details of these initiatives are gathered together in Appendix C, which forms a substantive part of this report and which we hope will be of practical use to readers. The list of examples is by no means exhaustive, and the examples themselves are not case studies but rather pointers for readers to follow up for themselves; to this end, Appendix C includes contact names from whom further information may be obtained.

Examples have been selected from a range of libraries in various parts of the country and from differing local authority contexts. We wish to emphasise that the examples have not necessarily been included as representing 'exceptional practice' but are initiatives already taken which demonstrate what can be done in terms of strategy and practice.

1.6 Method of working

The Working Party met six times between March 1993 and September 1994.

Concurrent with the early compilation of reviews of user surveys and research, and of documentary sources on service provision, an information collection exercise was mounted to tap experience of library services for children and young people through the medium of their professional interest groups. A standard list of questions was prepared, based on the agreed terms of reference, and circulated to all groups with a direct concern in the subject area by members of the Working Party acting on behalf of them. Information was collected over the summer of 1993 and was then collated into a working paper which, along with the submissions received from invited bodies, formed the basis of evidence for our report. In addition to the six main meetings, the members of the Working Party divided into five sub-groups which met between October and December 1993 to consider the information thus far assembled, and to draw from it the key conclusions and recommendations that could usefully be made.

In February 1994, following consideration by a small representative sub-group of a draft for a final report, priority was given to preparation of a shorter paper setting out key conclusions and recommendations. This paper was debated and agreed by the full Working Party in March 1994, and was subsequently circulated for comment to those professional interest groups that had contributed information in summer 1993.

The paper also formed the foundation for the full report. Following the March meeting, a further small sub-group was set up to assist the Secretary in preparing a draft of the full final report, and in identifying and selecting the examples of service initiatives referred to in 1.5 above. This last sub-group met twice, in June and July 1994. The resultant draft final report, together with the results of the summer consultation exercise, was considered by the Working Party at its final meeting on 21 September 1994.

All views expressed at the final meeting, and those submitted by professional bodies, were taken into account in formulating the final version of the Working Party's report, which was submitted to the Library and Information Services Council (England) on 3 November 1994.

References

1. LIBRARY AND INFORMATION SERVICES COUNCIL (England). *School libraries: the foundation of the curriculum.* HMSO, 1984. Library information series no.13.
2. LIBRARY ASSOCIATION. *Children and young people: Library Association guidelines for public library services.* Library Association Publishing Ltd, 1991.
3. LIBRARY AND INFORMATION STATISTICS UNIT. *A survey of library services to schools and children in the UK 1992/93* by Helen Pickering and John Sumsion. Loughborough University of Technology, 1993.

2 The needs of children and young people

Our main focus has been the user – children and young people between the ages of 0 and 16. We believe that the needs of the individuals within this group for books, for libraries and for encouragement of reading and the use of information, should be the starting point for any consideration of library services delivered to them, whether through public libraries, schools library services, school libraries or other channels, and that **recognition of these needs should inform and determine the aims and objectives of all libraries that serve this client group**.

It would be a mistake to regard children and young people as a homogeneous group. Needs for, and expectations of, a library service are conditioned by age, developmental stage, ability, the special needs of disadvantaged or minority groups, and by conditioning factors such as home circumstances or distance from a library. It is important that the public library in particular, which caters for all age groups, should be able to recognise the different needs arising at different ages and stages of development and should strive to satisfy these in appropriate ways.

2.1 Reading needs

There is a distinction between what children and young people **need**, and what they **want**, in terms of books and other types of reading material.

The fundamental need is for children to learn to read. To do this successfully, research has shown that key factors include being read to and the availability and experience of a wide range of books and stories.[1] The ability to acquire literacy and develop that skill does not come in the same way or at the same age for every child. This means that what has been termed 'high interest, low ability material' can be required into the teenage years. On the path to literacy children and their parents and carers need choices and informed guidance to suitable and enjoyable reading.

In general, needs between the ages of 5 and 16 are largely dictated by the formal education system. Children and young people need materials and services to support their formal education and their self-development and improvement in reading and information skills. The materials are those prescribed by the National Curriculum; the services are those, such as teaching in information skills, that are provided by the school according to its perception of need and its ability or inclination to devote staff time to it.

Wants are largely dictated by self-interest, the desire for informal education and information, the search for enjoyment. There are significant differences between what children want to read, and see as worth reading, and what adults expect them to read. Research conducted by WH Smith at various times has demonstrated the differences quite clearly; research by the BBC and the Red House Children's Book Club in 1990 into parents' attitudes towards children's books found that 40% of parents disliked or disapproved of some of the books their children enjoyed; more recent research by WH Smith jointly with HarperCollins into children's book purchasing indicates a clear difference between what adults think children should read and what they themselves want to.

Public Lending Right figures provide the most conclusive evidence of the continuing popularity of authors such as Dahl, Blyton and the Ahlbergs, all with over one million library loans in 1992. The overwhelming popularity of Dahl was confirmed by the analysis of favourite books at all ages from 6 to 12 done by Gallup in 1992, and by the Children's Reading Books for Pleasure survey carried out for Smarties in 1990. Knowledge of other authors may or may not be limited. The Smarties survey reported that 22 authors were mentioned without prompting, whereas the 1992 Gallup poll found that two-thirds of the 21 authors being promoted during Children's Book Week raised "scarcely a flicker of recognition". Most recently, a survey of primary school children in the London Borough of Southwark confirmed the popularity of the top three authors but also revealed a surprising range of authors read by children in the 5 to 11 age range, with girls ranging much more widely than boys.

Much effort has been devoted in recent decades to research which has attempted, by one methodology or another and at national or local level, to identify what children's real demands are for books or other forms of reading material (magazines, newspapers, etc.) and what particular factors make a 'reading child'.

The difficulties of surveying young people, and particularly young children, are well-known and well-recorded: the need for different questions for different age groups, the existence of factors that condition children's ability to use facilities such as libraries and bookshops – such as physical and financial constraints and difficulty of access. Apart from the problem of very young children who cannot properly speak for themselves but can only reply through the possibly distorting intermediary of a parent or carer, and of older children who may have various reasons for not replying responsibly to a survey, there is the major factor that children's replies are in all cases conditioned by their experience of what is available to them, and possibly by low expectations. The thoughts of the children themselves are notoriously difficult to research because of the strict guidelines concerning parental permission and accompaniment. We have noted, however, the advent of 'pester power', or children's ability to pester parents into buying certain products, which has aroused increased interest in children in the marketing world and resulted in more research studies conducted directly with children. (See also 4.1.8, 5.3.4).

2.2 Library needs

There is also a distinction between reading needs and wants (in total, reading demand) and library demand. Research into the library needs, or demand, of children and young people tends to be carried out by or for libraries. It normally focuses on existing use with the objective of extrapolating this into some assessment of needs; it often fails to include non-users; and it frequently concentrates on a specific age group. Its challenge is to identify what particular factors make a 'library-using child'.

Numerous public libraries have carried out surveys of use and demand in the whole or parts of their area, normally focusing on specific age groups, or have run promotions with before and after assessments. Most libraries seem to regard their findings as helpful in identifying trends, highlighting areas of demand, revealing attitudes to changes, showing lack of awareness of services and facilities, etc, and most have acted on them by developing service priorities and action plans, setting targets, incorporating findings in service specifications, and by practical measures such as boosting stock, adapting or introducing services, improving guiding, etc. Most libraries report increased use by the target group.

Waltham Forest Libraries and Arts Department
Teenagers and Libraries: a Study in Waltham Forest

Southwark Library Services
Survey of Primary School Children in the Borough

Other public libraries that have surveyed young users include
Dorset, Westminster, Nottinghamshire, Camden, Ealing,
Hertfordshire, and most recently Birmingham, in 1993

Not all research is done with a view to action. It may be done to confirm existing policies and practices, or to enable fine-tuning; it may be done for political advantage, to demonstrate efficiency or user satisfaction. Resources are therefore not necessarily critical to the achievement of desired ends. Most research is done, however, to assess: user satisfaction with existing services and preferred service options for the future; demand for facilities or for services that do not currently exist; effectiveness of promotions in terms of use; and the likely impact of new developments such as charging for overdue material, with a view to implementing whatever the findings are. Many surveys of library use by children and young people are carried out by individual libraries as part of their continuous monitoring of services, the results normally being fed into policy-making for service delivery. (See also 5.3.4).

In our investigation of information on children's reading and library needs, we have become aware that a great deal of time is wasted by individual libraries in either re-inventing wheels or in trying to ascertain what has gone before. Certainly there are local and national networks, but these are restricted to specialist interests and in general do not overlap. **There appears to be no regular or systematic mechanism through which information on local experience can be exchanged, or through which local libraries can gain information about research at national level.**

2.3 Factors affecting needs

In recognising the distinction between needs and wants (which in total equal demand) libraries have to balance the provision of material that will attract young people into the library with their responsibility to promote good quality material and to help in the development of reading ability and of appreciation of quality. They also have to balance the demands of children for material and information to support their school work with their demands for recreational material, in neither case necessarily confined to the printed book.

In addition, there are many factors in modern life which can influence what children need and what they want, and which in turn can have an impact on the provision of library services, particularly by the public library. The impact is seen in the extra pressure being placed on static or diminishing resources in public libraries in many parts of the country, leading to reconsideration of priorities in allocation of resources and targeting of services.

2.3.1 Educational factors

- The National Curriculum has introduced targeting of aspects of a subject, emphasis on project work, and the need for training in information skills, all of which have affected the reading and information materials required and the ways in which they are used.

- Local management of schools, by delegating budgets to individual schools, has had an impact on the standards of library provision in schools, and on the continuing ability of schools library services to provide support; this in turn may create a demand from school pupils for materials and assistance from public library services to counteract under-provision in their own institutions.

- Emphasis in schools on computer literacy and on multimedia study has widened the demands made by secondary school children, in particular, for material other than books and for public libraries to keep pace with IT developments and products.

These three factors, but especially the first two in combination, have a direct impact on services provided by public and school libraries and schools library services in the type of material they will be required to stock and in particular the multiplicity of copies of individual titles to cope with simultaneous demand. Individual schools may be unable, or unwilling, to support these demands from their own budgets, and they may be unable or unwilling to buy in services from the schools library services. This will drive motivated pupils to the public library for assistance (see also 5.6.4).

2.3.2 Recreational and leisure trends

- The growing popularity, particularly among young people over 12, of video games, 24-hour television, and other sophisticated leisure activities, together with the commercial hard sell and media hype attached to these, is reflected in a declining interest in reading in the teenage years, particularly among boys, and consequently a falling off in library use in this age group.

This factor impacts on public libraries, which have demonstrated a growing awareness that teenagers have different and quite separate needs from those of both younger children and adults although not all of them have been able to devote resources to surveying and identifying teenage needs, nor to making adequate provision for them (but see 5.6.7). There is an awareness that promotional activities have to compete for attention with the attractions of commercial operators, and that public libraries cannot in most cases match the ambience of commercial entertainment premises. In making provision for these promotional activities, public libraries have to weigh up the competing requirements of different age groups (in the context of competition from other client groups within the community) and allocate priorities amongst them for service targeting in conformity with library policy and council preferences.

2.3.3 Technological developments

- Development of more, and more sophisticated, IT sources, with packaging and information in a variety of formats.

Children and young people are becoming accustomed to multimedia packaging, information on CD-Rom, and computers for a variety of uses. Libraries in schools already provide a range of formats, and schools library services have to provide likewise in order to support them. Public libraries have to widen their range of material and invest in technology in order to compete (see 5.6.9) and this may mean reallocation of priorities within the materials fund. Service provision has to recognise that children are becoming increasingly computer literate, and have high expectations regarding the use of computers in libraries and instant personal access to information.

2.3.4 Social factors

- Children, particularly the very young, are vulnerable and dependent.
- Changing family structures, particularly when allied to poverty, may result in lack of privacy for children to study at home.
- The increase in unemployment among young people in many areas can lead to an increase in leisure time.

Young children have a unique dependence on carers to visit the library and therefore their access to facilities is determined by the leisure and work patterns of adults. There is also concern for the safety of children in public places.

Lack of study facilities among school children leads to pressure on public libraries to provide homework space after school hours, and areas where children can work undisturbed.

The third of the above factors can produce a greater demand for library facilities; it certainly offers the public library a role as provider of information on benefits, training opportunities, and other areas of likely interest to unemployed teenagers. Unemployed teenagers taking advantage of training opportunities are also likely to be thrown into reliance on the public library as an informal means of studying.

Key conclusions

- Recognition of the needs of children and young people for books, for libraries and for encouragement of reading and the use of information should inform and determine the aims and objectives of all libraries that serve this client group. [Section 2 introduction]

See also 5.3.2, which reiterates this Conclusion and from which Recommendation 4 flows

- There is at present no effective national networking of research information and other data relating to the reading and library needs of children and young people. [2.2]

Recommendation

■ There should be further investigation into how research and data relating to children's and young people's reading and library needs can be most effectively disseminated nationally. A national body such as the Library Association, with its specialist groups, should investigate the feasibility of an annual digest of information. [2.1, 2.2]

    – Library Association

References

1. For example, SMITH, Frank. *Reading*; 2nd edition. Cambridge UP, 1985. MEEK, Margaret. *How texts teach what readers learn*. Stroud, Glos., Thimble Press, 1988.

3 Books, reading and libraries: a reaffirmation of values

3.1 The importance of reading

Books are among the most important elements in the development of a child. The ability to read, along with the ability to spell and to write, **is** literacy. Reading contributes directly to the ability to spell and to write. The skill of reading, if acquired and encouraged in the early years of a child's development, and maintained through the teenage years into adulthood, lays the foundation for educational support, for the ability to find information, and for a lifetime of leisure enjoyment.

It has been proven beyond doubt that children who are encouraged to read in their pre-school and early school years, by parents and carers in the home, by teachers, and by librarians in the school and the local public library, have a considerable advantage in terms of educational performance and later achievement over those who have not been provided with these opportunities. For example,

- A survey of 9 to 13-year-olds in 20 countries carried out by the International Assessment of Educational Progress showed that in virtually all cases there was a positive correlation between both the number of books in the home and the amount of leisure reading, and educational attainment at school.[1]

- A report to the Lothian Regional Council Education Committee in December 1993 noted that "extensive worldwide research has identified the roots of successful literacy as lying in the early experiences of the child" and states that "experience with texts and stories in the home during the pre-school years is considered to be an essential preparation for literacy in all young children, and the lack of such experiences is a root factor in later literacy failure and under-achievement in otherwise normally-developing children".[2]

- The National Literacy Association, set up in 1991 in response to mounting concern about literacy, and supported by some 50 organisations including all the teaching unions, aims "to promote the view, and render it indisputable, that **every** child who is failing to acquire the basic skills of reading, writing and spelling, for whatever reason, is a cause for concern and that we must have the national will to address the problem". The Association's '99 by 99' campaign was launched in July 1993 with the aim of ensuring that 99% of children leave school with adequate literacy for living and working by 1999. The Association's overall policy, and a priority aim of the campaign, is to ensure a good supply of children's books to all households with children, and to schools.

- The Newspaper Society has launched the Newspapers in Education (NiE) initiative to promote reading of newspapers among young people as present and future readers. (For some children, a newspaper may be the only reading material in the home). Through NiE, regional newspapers are actively working with teachers, parents and pupils to promote a better understanding of the print media and an enthusiasm for the working of the newspaper; a main element of NiE is the use of the newspaper as a valuable, fun and real-life resource in the classroom to teach subjects across the curriculum.

- John Clare, Education Editor of the *Daily Telegraph*, wrote in a special report to coincide with Children's Book Week in October 1992 that "we know that children who do not begin to read freely and eagerly when they are young perform less well than their more literate peers throughout their school lives. They tend to end up among the bottom 40%, that stubbornly constant proportion who leave school at 16 with not much to show for 11 years of full-time education".

3.2 Perceptions of the importance of reading

We have noted above that the critical stages of a child's life in which books should be introduced, and reading encouraged, are the pre-school and early school years. We have also noted evidence that the availability of books and story-telling in the home has a direct influence on the child's ability to read. Parental perceptions are thus particularly important in establishing the basis of literacy at an early age, as is the attitude of schools towards parental involvement in the teaching and learning process.

- A survey carried out in 1989 among 500 adult members of the Red House Children's Book Club found that only 44% of the parents said that their child's school was in favour of their helping their child to learn to read at home, though 57% were in favour for four- and five-year-olds; but 21% of parents reported that their school explicitly discouraged their help, the figure rising to 28% among parents of five-year-olds.

- The National Literacy Trust, an independent charity established in October 1993 to help improve reading and writing standards in the UK, with its key focus on families and how it can support parents in their efforts to help their children to read and explore the printed word, commissioned research into the general public's attitudes to and feelings about reading and writing. It found that:

  - 84% of adults would be willing to give up some of their time, in partnership with schools, to help their children to read;

  - 96% of adults believe that individual help and encouragement from parents are critical to a child's development throughout school life;

  - adults still think the ability to read and write is more important than the ability to use computers, and that reading is more important than writing;

  - 79% think reading will be just as or more important in the future as it is now.

But there is conflicting evidence.

- A Gallup poll in 1992 found that 35% of children aged between 6 and 12 read little or nothing for pleasure; 24% of parents read no books for their own enjoyment in an average year; 44% of parents never read to their children.

The Working Party is in no doubt about the importance and the value of books and reading for children and young people. But we are concerned that they are in danger because of:

- Government policies with regard to the teaching of reading, plus the demands of the National Curriculum;

- competititon from alternative recreational opportunities;

- competition from information technology in schools.

3.3   The literacy problem in the UK

Despite the facts set out in the preceding pages, and despite acknowledgement from many source of the direct link between literacy and other basic skills and the competitiveness of the UK in business and industry, the problem of literacy has yet to be solved.

- Surveys by the Adult Literacy and Basic Skills Unit show that:
  - one-third of 14-year-olds have a reading age of 11 or less;
  - 6.5 million, or one in eight of over 16s, have serious difficulties in reading, writing, understanding or speaking English;
  - 40% of 16 to 19-year-olds in further education lack basic literacy and numeracy skills.

- A report by Ernst & Young for the National Book Committee found that:
  - the UK ranks 20 out of 22 OECD countries in the degree to which its education system meets the needs of a competitive economy: poor basic skills mean that our young people are ill-equipped to meet the requirements of business;
  - 61% of jobs require reasonable reading skills; 45% of UK companies state that reading skills have become more important;
  - the cost to UK business of poor basic skills may be £8.4 billion a year (ALBSU);
  - the economic and social benefits of promoting literacy, including access to books, could be worth over £10 billion a year.[3]

Numerous studies have found a causal relationship between social and economic disadvantage and lack of reading ability in children and young people, carrying on into adulthood. For example:

- A report to Lothian Regional Council Education Committee in December 1993[4] based on a study of five schools in the region, of which one served an area of "comparative socio-economic advantage", found that in the "advantaged" area, the percentage of eight-year-olds with a reading age of below five years nine months, was zero; in the other four schools it ranged from 26.3% to 52.3%. The study also found a difference, which could not be accounted for merely by teaching methods, between children from homes where there were books and discussion and those where these were unfamiliar.[4]

- Data from the National Child Development Study demonstrates a direct relationship between parents with reading difficulties and children with the lowest levels of basic skills, especially in low-income families.

13

The Adult Literacy and Basic Skills Unit has said that:

> "We believe that breaking the cycle of reading failure is urgent. We can't afford to leave it much longer. The cost of poor basic skills is increasingly clear. It costs the individual in missed opportunities, it costs industry in lack of competitiveness and unnecessary waste; it costs our future in lost potential."[5]

3.4 Reading habits and patterns

In the preceding sections we have noted some of the factors that influence a child's ability to read. Ability alone will not make a reader, though it is one of the factors that influence reading for enjoyment.

- The factors affecting propensity to read that emerge from numerous surveys include:
  - social class: children with fathers in non-manual occupations read more books than those with fathers in manual occupations;
  - gender: girls read more than boys;
  - ability and attainment as assessed by the school: the higher the ability, the more children tend to read books; conversely, difficulty in reading is a factor in tendency to avoid reading.

- It has also been found that a child was more likely **not** to be a reader through:
  - lack in the school of some form of positive encouragement to read;
  - lack of a class library, library lessons, silent reading periods, qualified librarian, school bookshop, or school book club.[6]

Again, there is conflicting evidence regarding the reading habits of young people.

- Surveys carried out over the past 20 years have consistently found:
  - a decline in reading as children, particularly boys, grow older, though there are fluctuations due to exams, holidays, etc;
  - television is a major challenge to reading as a leisure time pursuit;
  - reading as an activity has a negative image, particularly for boys.

The most recent evidence, from the pilot survey carried out in 1993 by the Children's Literature Research Centre as a preliminary to its full-scale mass survey of juvenile reading habits, indicates that substantially more boys in all age groups between 4 and 16 would rather play a new computer game than read a good book (or watch television); and that among girls, while those in the age groups 4 to 7 and 7 to 11 would prefer to read a book, those between 11 and 16 prefer to watch their favourite programmes on television.[7]

Despite these survey findings, there is evidence of the continuing popularity and dominance of the book for reading through both purchase and borrowing.

More than 7,000 children's books were published in 1993. Between 1985 and 1990 sales of children's books increased by 170% (corresponding adult book sales rose by 47%) and 150 million children's books are now sold every year. However, as the Children's Literature Research Centre points out, this "is not indicative of improvements in children's reading abilities; neither is it necessarily a sign of increased interest in books for children on the part of publishers except in so far as they are saleable commodities. Indeed, children's reading has become the site of many competing social pressures which have very little to do with the relationship between the child and the book".[8]

The significance of children as borrowers is demonstrated by statistics for 121 authorities in England and Wales, which show a steady rise in children's stock holdings and in items borrowed in both public libraries and in schools library services, with a particularly dramatic increase in items borrowed by children from public libraries.

Public library services for children

	1992-93	1991-92	1990-91
Stock	22.5 million items	21.7 million	20.7 million
Issues	101 million items	95.5 million	82 million

Schools library services

	1992-93	1991-92	1990-91
Stock	28.4 million items	25.6 million	25.2 million
Issues per year	16 million items	15.8 million	14.8 million
Loans in schools	20 million items	20 million	18.4 million

3.5 The role of the library

One of the critical factors in the encouragement of reading among children and young people is that books should be both available and accessible: available in the sense of being in places where children can get at them, accessible in the sense that any child, either independently or through intermediary help and guidance, can use them.

Books are available through a number of channels such as bookshops and book clubs, and guidance to the wealth of published children's books is available in specialist magazines such as *Books for keeps*. These facilities are not necessarily accessible to all. Many areas are poorly provided with bookshops, and specialist children's bookshops are confined to a minority of areas; cost can also be a deterrent to book purchase. Book clubs and specialist magazines require knowledge of their existence on the part of parents, and interest to pursue them; they are not immediately and easily accessible to the majority.

Public libraries are the only means whereby the widest choice of titles can be made available free of charge to the user. They also have, or should have, the means of making books accessible to children through display, promotion, advice and assistance. They are the one potentially constant source of supply of books which can also provide an environment in which to enjoy reading and gain value from it.

As the Book Trust report *Books in schools* observes:

"Public libraries are vital for giving children easy and free access to a wide range of books, forming the basis for a lifetime's use and enjoyment. It offers them the freedom to browse and to choose for themselves. In teaching information skills and the subject courses, most schools require pupils of all ages to use sources outside the school. They should have to search for and assess the information sources as they will have to in their adult working and personal life. The public library is central to this."[9]

Of the impact of a good library in the school on educational achievement, there is also evidence. For example:

● A study in Colorado, USA in 1991/92 provides evidence of the positive impact of library media centres on academic achievement in 221 Colorado public schools. This study was unusual in taking the school rather than the student as the unit for analysis, considering service outputs as well as resource inputs, and ruling out the effects of selected school and community conditions. It found that:
  – where centres are better funded, academic achievement is higher, whether their schools and communities are rich or poor and whether adults in the community are well or poorly educated;
  – better funding for centres fosters academic achievement by providing students with access to more library media staff and larger and more varied collections;
  – students whose library media specialists participate in the instructional process are higher academic achievers;
  – among predictors of academic achievement, the size of the centre staff and collection is second only to the absence of at-risk conditions, particularly poverty and low educational attainment among adults; in other words, at-risk factors exert the greatest influence on academic achievement (pulling it down) but the size of the library media center staff and collection is the only other factor that affects achievement (pushing it up).[10]

Conversely, numerous reports by HM Inspectors of schools throughout England and Wales testify that where library provision and use is poor, pupils' abilities in information handling and research and study skills are correspondingly under-developed. Absence within a school of positive encouragement to read has, as was noted above, a deleterious effect on a child's propensity to read.

On the basis of all the foregoing evidence, **it is our clear view that, at a time when unfulfilled reading potential affects the economic, cultural and social life of the country, the potential of a library, and in particular the public library which is freely available to all, as a force in support of reading and information literacy cannot be too strongly emphasised**. By making books available to all who want them, together with specialist staff to make them accessible through advice and assistance in the choice and use of them, libraries are uniquely placed to make a significant contribution to the encouragement of reading among children and young people.

In view of this conclusion, it is a matter of considerable concern that this unique force appears to have been overlooked or at least marginalised by those agencies set up to study and combat illiteracy. The place of the public library in getting books to children, either directly or through parents or carers, is hardly mentioned. Clearly there has been a failure to communicate the potential of the public library in this respect.

In part this must be due to the library profession's age-old inability to promote itself and its services in places that matter. In this respect, **it suffers from the absence of a single national representative forum for the interests of**

children and young people in relation to libraries and information services that could act as a channel of communication with agencies such as the National Literacy Trust and the National Literacy Association.

In part, also, we suspect that there is a lack of hard evidence, drawn from well-conducted research, to demonstrate unequivocally:

- that reading and library use make significant impacts on the personal, economic and educational achievement of children and young people, enabling the individual to make valuable and life-long contributions to society;
- that there are positive and wide-reaching benefits arising from the constructive use of leisure time in reading.

These impacts and benefits should be explored through well-constructed research, complemented by studies that approach the issues from the child's perspective.

Key conclusions

● Public libraries are the only means whereby the widest choice of titles can be made available free of charge to the user. They also have, or should have, the means of making books accessible to children through display, promotion, advice and assistance. They are the one potentially constant source of supply of books which can also provide an environment in which to enjoy reading and gain value from it. [3.5]

● At a time when unfulfilled reading potential affects the economic, cultural and social life of the country, the potential of a library, and in particular the public library which is freely available to all, as a force in support of reading and information literacy cannot be too strongly emphasised. [3.5]

● The library profession suffers from the absence of a single national representative forum for the interests of children and young people in relation to libraries and information services that could act as a channel of communication with agencies such as the National Literacy Trust and the National Literacy Association. [3.5]

● The impacts and benefits of reading and library use on the development of young people should be explored through well-constructed research, complemented by studies that approach the issues from the child's perspective. [3.5]

Recommendations

■ When the Federation of Local Authority Chief Librarians (FOLACL) supersedes its present constituent organisations in 1996 as a single representative body for chief librarians, the opportunity should be taken to merge the existing specialist groups, Association of Metropolitan District Chief Librarians, Society of County Children's and Education Librarians, and Youth and Education Librarians London, into a similar single forum. [3.5]

– FOLACL

■ Priority should be given to research which explores the benefits, impacts and effectiveness of library provision for children and young people. [3.5]

   – BL; DNH (Library and Information Commission); Research Bodies; FOLACL Public Library Research Group

References

1. Quoted in ERNST & YOUNG. *Literacy, education and training, their impact on the UK economy: report to the National Book Committee.* Ernst & Young, 1993.
2. LOTHIAN REGIONAL COUNCIL EDUCATION COMMITTEE. *Deprivation, early intervention and the prevention of reading difficulties: a review of initiatives and policy developments in Lothian Edinburgh, Lothian RC, 1993.*
3. ERNST & YOUNG *op. cit.*
4. LOTHIAN REGIONAL COUNCIL EDUCATION COMMITTEE *op. cit.*
5. ADULT LITERACY AND BASIC SKILLS UNIT. *Annual report 1992/93.* ALBSU, 1993.
6. HEATHER, P. *Young people's reading.* Sheffield, Centre for Research in User Studies, 1981. CRUS Occasional Paper 6, BLR&DD Report 5650.
7. CHILDREN'S LITERATURE RESEARCH CENTRE. *Contemporary juvenile reading habits: a study of young people's reading at the end of the century.* Roehampton Institute, CLRC, 1994.
8. CHILDREN'S LITERATURE RESEARCH CENTRE *op. cit.*
9. BOOK TRUST. *Books in schools.* Book Trust, 1992. Book Trust Report 1, British National Bibliography Research Fund Report 60.
10. LANCE, Keith Curry, WELBORN, Lynda, and HAMILTON-PENNELL, Christine. *The impact of school media centers on academic achievement.* Castle Rock, Colorado, Hi Willow Research and Publishing, 1993.

4 Libraries meeting needs: the current situation

The Working Party, relying on evidence from its members and the organisations that they represent, from the library profession through various channels, and from organisations with an interest in the area, has identified the major concerns of the current situation as:

- funding levels of libraries in all sectors providing service to children and young people;

- wide variations in the standard of services in all sectors, not necessarily arising from variations in funding levels;

- inequality of access, arising largely from the above two factors.

With regard to public library services for children and young people in particular, there are major concerns regarding:

- education, training and continuing professional development;

- staffing and status of children's services.

The Working Party is also concerned specifically with:

- the future of schools library services.

Although the Working Party does not believe that a crisis exists at present in any of the sectors that it has considered, it does see evidence of a range of developing factors such as contracting out and local government reform which could impact on the current situation.

4.1 Public library services for children and young people

4.1.1 Present structures

Services for children and young people provided by public libraries have been the principal focus of our attention. They form the pervasive element in services for young people, being the only service to embrace not just the educational but also the recreational and information and cultural needs of children and young people, and to be available to all age groups. It is the only statutory library service that is available to pre-school children, the 'under-five' age group, where introduction to books and the pleasure of reading is crucial.

The provision of a public library service by local authorities throughout the UK is required or enabled by statute, although the legislative base differs from one country to another. The nature and extent of the service is not prescribed; it is only required (in England and Wales) that an authority shall provide a 'comprehensive and efficient service'. The definition of that phrase has exercised minds for many years, but has come into sharper focus in the recent context of contracting out, and charging for, services. In tandem with this, uncertainty has arisen, not least through ministerial statements, as to the extent of the 'core' service that should continue to be free of charge. The place of services for children and young people within these areas has never been defined.

A review carried out by consultants during 1994 has examined public library services currently provided by local authorities in England and Wales, together with the working of the 1964 Public Libraries and Museums Act, and the changing environment within which libraries have to operate. This is the first major review of the public library service since the McColvin Report in 1942, and its research has revealed the "strong feelings expressed about the importance of the public library for children and young people" and "an investment in the young at the head of a list of prime purposes at the core of public library provision".[1]

The outcome of the review will be a strategic approach for the public library service of the future, including guidelines and a framework for local choice on what constitutes a comprehensive and efficient service and how it can best be delivered. **The Working Party wishes the review team to recognise the need to reinforce the statutory responsibility of local library authorities to address the needs of children as individuals as firmly integral to, and at the core of, public library services, and to accept its recommendations in pursuit of that end**.

4.1.2 Funding

Funding levels are cause for concern in a significant number of areas of the country and reflect the continuing pressure from central government to restrain local authority expenditure. Few public libraries are not susceptible to at least the threat of budget cuts or restraint affecting all or some areas of their services. Charge capping and exceeding the statutory spending allowance (SSA) are an ever-present threat or reality for most authorities. Internally, however, the size of the budget allocated to services for children and young people is as likely to reflect the perceived status and importance of these services, and the priority attached to them in the context of the needs of other client groups, as it is to be dictated by overall financial constraint.

The most recent edition of the annual *Public libraries and their book funds*, which analyses year-on-year spending on books by public libraries, finds that overall levels of public library spending on books in all parts of the United Kingdom are "disturbingly low", and that there are huge disparities in levels of real purchase between authorities. The report measures expenditure for 1991/92 against the base of 1981/82 (a base of very low expenditure) and finds that spending has barely kept above the Retail Price Index and has declined against the Book Index: the purchasing power of book funds is therefore still falling.[2]

These remarks refer to public library spending overall. The difficulty of calculating precise or even notional figures for expenditure on public library services for children and young people is acknowledged. The figures used by the Library and Information Statistics Unit (LISU) are based on children's services for the age range 0 to 14. Beyond that age, the majority of library authorities regard users as adult (see also 1.4). Young people of 14 and over use the full range of public library services, perhaps particularly, for those in the final stages of formal education, the reference and local studies collections; it is also possible that teenagers of limited reading ability use sections of the public library set aside for younger children.

The most recent published survey from LISU, for 1992/93, notes "an upward trend in the public library service to children, particularly in Scotland and in London": figures for the last five years of materials funds give a general impression of increased spending from year to year. "However, there are enough cases of a reverse trend to justify the anxiety felt in the book trade, among educationalists and by librarians in the authorities concerned." Comparing figures for 1992/93 with those projected for 1993/94, some 28% of authorities "report a declining materials fund in 1993/94. In particular, several of the English metropolitan authorities are experiencing such falls".[3]

National statistics show that there are wide variations in the budgets allocated to services for children amongst local authorities in different parts of the country.[4] Our view is that it is inappropriate to specify a minimum level of expenditure for universal application to all library authorities. We believe that a **percentage of the _total_ materials budget should be applied to services for children and young people, and that the percentage should be _at least_ the percentage of children and young people in the population served. The percentage should be determined locally and should be subject to regular review**.

4.1.3 Standards

We are concerned at the very wide range of standards which is apparent in children's services in public libraries all over the country. This is true also of public libraries in general. The preliminary findings of the review of the public library service in England and Wales commissioned by the Department of National Heritage reveal "considerable variations in the quality of public library services across the country". In pointing this out, the review also "raises the question of how to define and raise standards, when the best [authorities] confine their activities to their own bailiwick and the worst encounter few challenges".[5]

That there are wide variations in standards of service provision is undeniable. **While quality is not exclusively a product of funding, the ability to meet high standards of service does depend on adequate funding**. Standards have fallen because reduced budgets cannot support former excellence. Standards within individual services are dictated partly by funding levels but also – and perhaps more potently – by internal priorities in the allocation of budgets, management perceptions of the importance of the library, and the quality of staff whose function it is to observe and maintain specified standards. In general, published national standards and guidelines are at best regarded as targets, at worst ignored. They cannot be enforced. It may be that the notion of 'benchmarks' – which we define as examples of initiatives in strategy or practice to which all can aspire – is more realistic and capable of application than national standards which can in any case be regarded as minimum requirements and can be as much a tool for levelling down as one for levelling up. In some respects, standards have been replaced or supplemented by the notion of user entitlement, manifested in customer charters both national and local. (See also 5.3.1)

The Department of National Heritage has a superintending role *vis-a-vis* public libraries in England: the Secretary of State has a responsibility for ensuring that each local authority in England complies with its statutory requirement to provide a 'comprehensive and efficient' library service, and the power to enforce that requirement if an authority is seen to be conspicuously failing in its duty. The power of enforcement has been used very sparingly, because there is no formal systematic programme of inspection to ensure that standards are being maintained; there are differing interpretations of 'comprehensive and efficient'; there are no national standards against which an authority can be seen to be performing at a very low level.

The Department has consulted all English library authorities on a proposed methodology for assessing their performance of their statutory duties. Responses to the consultation are currently being analysed and an announcement is expected. The intention is to have an agreed methodology in place in time to inform the thinking of any new library authorities which emerge from the review of local government in the English counties. **We should like to see any monitoring or assessment procedures for public libraries make explicit reference to children's services.**

4.1.4 Equality of access

Access to libraries and to books in general is, and always has been, unequal. But it is obvious that inequality has been exacerbated by cuts in budgets leading to children (and their parents and carers) being denied access through reduced opening hours and in some areas closure of service points. Overall, inequality of access has a geographical distribution, though problems of access are not confined to remote rural areas but can be equally a feature of urban life.

Total equality of access is unrealistic throughout all parts of the country, but a minimum level of access is essential for children in particular, who are liable to disadvantage through physical, social and legal factors such as distance, opening hours, dependence on carers, and absence of supervision. Not all libraries can make available all the material that children want. But they can provide access to it. Libraries must be gateways to the resources of other libraries, local, regional and national, and these gateways must be equally accessible to all. But so must the resources. It is of particular concern to us that the present inability to obtain material for children through the national interlending system serves to extend the problem of inequality.

The concept of the library gateway as a key element in service equalisation was emphasised in the Department of National Heritage report *Library and information provision in rural areas in England and Wales* and **we support its recommendation to library managers that they should "make special efforts to maintain and, where possible, develop library and information services aimed at rurally-based children to assist their educational development and provide literacy, leisure and information support".**[6]

4.1.5 Staffing and status of children's services

Traditionally, within the public library, the service to children and the service to schools have been co-ordinated through the medium of a single professional post in charge of both. In recent years, there has been the beginning of a discernible trend towards separation of services to children and services to schools, sometimes without a single professional in charge of both. Overall, however, within those public library services that continue to operate the schools library service, a total of 88 joint responsibility posts remain. Representation at senior management level of these posts has declined, from 18 in 1991/92 to 13 in 1992/93.[7]

The perceived advantage of joint responsibility posts at senior level has been that of integrating the schools library service into the work of the library department overall. In recent years, this has come to be seen as not entirely advantageous. The emphasis of schools library service staff expertise has moved from knowledge of children's books to knowledge of the curriculum, and the community of interest has lessened; and as demands from schools grew and the schools library service began to require increasing attention, tensions between the two wings of the service arose. The Library and Information Statistics Unit statistics have noted a significant increase in the amount of time spent on schools in joint responsibility posts as opposed to children's services: in 1992/93, more time was spent on schools in 44 authorities, compared with 21 authorities in 1990/91.

That there are advantages and disadvantages is spelled out in *Children and young people: Library Association guidelines for public library services* which recommends co-ordination of the two services through a senior management post "with overall responsibility for co-ordinating, managing, developing and monitoring services to children and to education".[8]

Nationally, there is an increasing number of generalist posts in public libraries at all tiers of staffing. At senior management level, this is the result of library service integration into large directorates, and pressures in local government generally to rationalise and reduce senior management structures. There is also a requirement for individual librarians to accept responsibility for a wider range of services and to develop a broader range of skills. Increasingly, specialists with operational responsibility are not represented at senior management level. The draft report of the Department of National Heritage review of the public library service observes that "Such policies may well appear ill advised in the light of our findings".[9]

Whether such specialists are members of management teams or not, **it is essential that issues relating to services for children and young people continue to be properly represented and debated in senior management teams through a team member having a specific brief for this sector, and within the client team where a client/contractor situation exists. This will ensure that the management of services for children and young people remains fully integrated into public library management at the highest level, and dispel perceptions of marginalisation or separatism.**

4.1.6 Education and training of staff

There are now few specialist modules in children's librarianship and literature on offer in British Librarianship and Information Studies (LIS) schools, and there is little prospect that the general pattern at undergraduate level will change significantly in this respect. It has to be recognised that first professional education (now entirely within the university sector) provides a grounding through generic courses that emphasise the principles and skills common to all occupational sub-groups, and that this grounding must be built upon through in-service training and continuing professional development.

This pattern inevitably places more onus on individual public libraries to provide good quality in-service training for their staff, although it must be pointed out that the need for in-service training is not simply a product of generalist university education and that numerous libraries have recognised its importance for many years and have provided it either independently or in conjunction with other libraries.

Gwent Libraries
In-service and Co-operative Training

Yorkshire Children's Services Group

Greater Manchester Public Library Training Co-operative

To provide good quality services for children and young people, all staff who encounter children in the delivery of library services and all specialists working in those services must be committed to and motivated by the requirements of those clients, and should have adequate opportunities for specialist in-house training.

Specialist training must include:

— knowledge and understanding of the specific stock requirements of clients for their recreational and educational needs;

— ability to communicate effectively with clients, including the art of storytelling;

— ability to handle differently-sized groups of children and young people;

— knowledge of requirements of parents and carers of young children;

— skills in promotion of the service.

Of these, knowledge of children's books is, from the evidence, the critical issue. Staff must be motivated to read, know and enthuse about books. If the knowledge of, and enthusiasm for, books is not there, the service will assuredly dwindle.

Although there are few specialist modules on offer, there are still some (eg, at the University of Central England, and the University of Northumbria at Newcastle) and there remains considerable opportunity for students at all levels to undertake projects and research in aspects of children's or school librarianship or children's literature.

The major under-developed area in which LIS schools could usefully join with practitioners is that of continuing professional development. While some of the courses run by specialist professional groups are well-received, there is overall a lack of structure and consistent quality that belies the very strong professional commitment we have observed among children's and education librarians. A partnership between practitioners and LIS schools with interest and experience in this sector could assess needs and examine mechanisms for promoting a more structured, high quality continuing professional development programme targeted at those already working with, or interested in working with, children and young people.

4.1.7 Factors conditioning ability to meet needs

Funding

Funding overall, and funding priorities within local authorities, result in a continuing need to balance resources between sustaining existing services and introducing new ones, between existing and future needs, between different age groups and types of special needs, with either selective targeting or a thin spread over a wide area of needs. Better targeting of services through establishment of specific priorities, and better stock exploitation, are methods of counteracting the effects of cuts.

Specialist staff

Loss of specialist staff due to internal policies and/or staff restructuring may affect the ability to plan for proper client-focused services for children and young people. On the other hand, staff restructuring can provide opportunities for alternative styles of service delivery, with new ways of co-ordinating provision across the whole service, and specialist training for professional and paraprofessional staff.

Local government reform

Although the pattern to be imposed by reform in many counties of England has not yet been determined, it is clear that existing proposals would result in the dismemberment of some county authorities, with consequent dispersal of county library systems and their resources, loss of economies of scale in service delivery and fragmentation of existing services. (See also 4.3.3).

It is unlikely that all of the proposed new unitary authorities will have the resource base from which to operate effective library services to meet the educational, information and recreational needs of children and young people.

National Curriculum demands

Pressures caused by the short-term/high-volume demands arising from the National Curriculum can be a distorting factor for libraries struggling to meet the needs of all ages. Difficulties arise (even where the budget is sizeable) particularly in provision of non-fiction: the major difficulty is trying to provide sufficient material to meet homework demand when the same topic is being covered by a whole class or, in some cases, a number of classes or schools simultaneously. The forthcoming reduction in National Curriculum requirements will not lessen demand in this respect.

Inadequate education library provision

Allied to the specific demands of the National Curriculum, public libraries in numerous areas are experiencing additional demands through failure of local schools and colleges to provide adequate library resources themselves, such demand falling not only on the library's own stock and staff, but also on the regional and national interlending network. In the case of schools, there is the possibility that schools will look to the 'free' public library service as an alternative to the charged schools library service to augment their resources through extensive borrowing, heavy use of information services, and more frequent class visits. Evidence of this is noted in the recently-reported study of schools library services commissioned from Coopers & Lybrand by the Department of National Heritage which states: "This appears to be a growing phenomenon although we are not aware of any national statistical evidence which identifies its true scale".[10] (See also 5.2, 5.5)

4.1.8 Libraries meeting needs

The extent to which services meet needs is virtually impossible to quantify since there is no finite measure of need and no set of nationally accepted standards; needs vary from one authority to another, and change in accordance with factors such as demographic shifts and educational developments. Given the range of potential needs within the age range under consideration, response is inevitably inadequate even given reasonable funding and a strong commitment to the service. For any individual authority, it is a question of establishing policies and priorities in accordance with perceived community needs and authority culture, setting targets within these, and attempting to meet them.

Particular difficulty in meeting needs appears to be experienced in the metropolitan districts where a substantial majority have experienced budget cuts leading to reductions in book funds, staffing and opening hours, with knock-on effects on lack of specialist training for staff, reduction in promotional activities, lack of research into customer wants and needs. In London, although a few boroughs have experienced no (visible) cuts in services thus far, the majority of services are curtailed through restricted book funds, lack of staff, inadequate buildings, reduced opening hours, or combinations of these. The result is inability to provide material that is clearly in demand, specialist advice and assistance to children, space for homework and access at convenient times, and a full range of promotional activities. More counties are reasonably satisfied with their ability to meet needs than are not, although in most cases it is recognised that meeting all needs is not possible and that those that are met have to be met within available resources; among those that are not satisfied, staff are responding to rather than attempting to meet needs, or struggling to keep a worthwhile service going.

Despite widespread funding difficulties, there are numerous examples of individual libraries maintaining standards, providing effective services, and initiating developments, through a judicious combination of strategic management of cuts, reallocation of priorities, better targeting of services, and other measures.

Even in the English metropolitan districts, where budget cuts have bitten more deeply and more widely than in other authorities, there are still indications of children's use of the library holding up and even, in a few cases, a satisfactory situation in which most needs are at present met. There are opportunities, through Urban Programme funding, to meet the changing needs of inner city areas through initiatives such as building refurbishment to improve provision for under-fives, provision of multimedia resources, and involvement in literacy and educational development programmes. It is, however, our conclusion, based on the evidence available to us, that in the present economic climate, no public library is able to reach its full potential.

It is a fact that, nationally, children's book issues in public libraries have consistently remained steady or increased while issues of other categories have in most cases declined (see 3.4).

There has been, however, no properly structured, comprehensive, national survey of children's or young people's attitudes to and use of the public library service. A few national surveys have included one or two questions regarding library use as part of an attempt to identify leisure habits in general. The questionnaire for the pilot run of the mass survey of juvenile reading habits conducted by the Children's Literature Research Centre, contains use of libraries as one variable among several at some of its questions, but its principal focus is on the kind of books young people read, and why they read them. (See also 5.3.4).

The nearest it is possible to get to an up-to-date national picture is through the findings of the Library Association's survey of children aged 4 to 16 as part of the National Library Week promotion in November 1993. Questionnaires on library use were completed by 2,300 children as part of a competition promoting literacy called 'Check this out'. The results show that 70% of the 4- to 16-year-olds say they use their library once a fortnight or more, and 51% at least once a week, with 38% spending 15 to 30 minutes on a visit and 20% between 30 minutes and an hour. Satisfaction with library opening hours was high, with 70% saying their library was open when they wanted it to be.

While these figures are encouraging and allow the Library Association to claim that "Libraries are making a crucial contribution to the education and literacy levels of our children", it has to be said that this is not a representative sample of children at large, but a population of those who are already keen readers and who are sufficiently motivated to take part in a competition on literacy and reading; no analysis is available by age, although most of the returns came from children in the 9 to 13 age group.

More objective are the results from the pilot survey conducted by the Children's Literature Research Centre, covering 321 pupils at schools of different types in south east England, which show that in age groups 4 to 7 and 7 to 11, more children borrow books from their local library than from any other source, and in the 11 to 16 age group more than half borrow from their local library although borrowing from friends is more popular, particularly amongst girls (borrowing from the school library decreases with age for both boys and girls).[11] The mass survey, involving 8,000 questionnaires in 1994/95, should provide more conclusive evidence. (See also 5.3.4)

Key conclusions

- The Working Party wishes the consultants carrying out the Department of National Heritage review of the public library service to recognise the need to reinforce the statutory responsibility of local library authorities to address the needs of children as individuals as firmly integral to, and at the core of, public library services, and to accept its recommendations in pursuit of that end. [4.1.1]

- A percentage of the **total** materials budget should be applied to services for children and young people, that percentage being **at least** the percentage of children and young people in the population served. The percentage should be locally determined and subject to regular review. [4.1.2]

- While quality is not exclusively a product of funding, the ability to meet high standards of service does depend on adequate funding. [4.1.3]

- Monitoring and assessment procedures for public libraries should make explicit reference to children's services. [4.1.3]

- Total equality of access is unrealistic throughout all parts of the country, but a minimum level of access is essential for children, who are liable to disadvantage through physical, social and legal factors such as distance, opening hours, dependence on carers, and absence of supervision. [4.1.4]

- We support the recommendation to library managers from the DNH report on library and information provision in rural areas in England and Wales, that they should "make special efforts to maintain and, where possible, develop library and information services aimed at rurally-based children to assist their educational development and provide literacy, leisure and information support". [4.1.4]

- It is essential that issues relating to services for children and young people continue to be properly represented and debated in senior management teams through a team member having a specific brief for this sector, or within the client team responsible for contracted-out services. This will ensure that the management of services for children and young people remains fully integrated into the public library management at the highest level, and dispel perceptions of marginalisation or separatism. [4.1.5]

- To provide good quality services for children and young people, all staff who encounter children in the delivery of library services and all specialists working in those services must be committed to and motivated by the requirements of those clients, and should have adequate opportunities for specialist in-house training. [4.1.6]

Recommendations

- The percentage of the **total** materials budget applied to services for children and young people should be determined locally and should be **at least** the same as the percentage of children and young people in the population served. [4.1.2]

  – Library Authorities; Library Managers

- The role of the Department of National Heritage in monitoring the whole public library service, and assessment procedures specified by it for this purpose, should include explicit reference to services for children and young people. [4.1.3]

  – DNH

- Every library authority should have a strategy to ensure and promote equal access to its resources for children and young people. [4.1.4]

  – Library Authorities; Library Managers

- The public library's senior management team (or equivalent) should include a person with designated overall responsibility for services for children and young people. [4.1.5]

  – Library Managers

■ Every library authority should have a strategy for specialist training of staff engaged in work with children and young people. [4.1.6]

– Library Authorities; Library Managers

4.2 School libraries

4.2.1 Current structures

In England and Wales, there is no statutory requirement for schools to have libraries, although the majority of them do have some measure of library provision. In Scotland and Northern Ireland, provision of libraries in schools is statutory.

Local Management of Schools (LMS) is producing a very varied pattern throughout England and Wales. In some local education authority (LEA) areas, a substantial number of schools have opted out of LEA control and now, as grant-maintained schools, draw their funding direct from central sources. In other areas, the majority of schools have elected to stay within LEA control, and their budgets are individually delegated by the LEA. The mix of LEA and grant-maintained schools is very different across England and Wales. The third element in the mix comprises the independent schools, the incidence of which has always varied from one part of the country to another.

Under LMS, budgets are delegated to schools by means of a formula drawn up by the LEA and approved by the Secretary of State: that formula determines the budget for each individual school. What, if any, part of the budget is spent on books is at the discretion of the head teacher and governing body. Grant-maintained schools likewise make their own decisions on what part of their own budget is spent on books or libraries, as do independent schools.

There is a view that LMS, by its fragmentation of responsibility for library expenditure amongst individual schools, runs counter to attempts to define coherent service objectives and standards for school libraries in general and to prepare integrated strategies for service delivery. This will be exacerbated when local government reform introduces more and smaller local authorities.

4.2.2 Funding

There are enormous variations in the resources devoted to libraries in individual schools, and in their staffing, and their use. These variations are not necessarily or exclusively the result of overall budget constraint, but may reflect the differing priorities attached by head teachers or governors to the importance of a library. Her Majesty's Inspectorate surveys of both primary and secondary schools in various parts of England have for many years drawn attention to disparities in library provision arising principally from differing priorities given by schools to library provision and book-buying policies. These reports point up the potential of inadequate library provision to undermine the validity of the National Curriculum.

Although there is a virtual absence of statistical information regarding the level and use of library provision in schools (see 4.4.2) bodies such as Book Trust and the Educational Publishers' Council have been active in recent years both in collecting evidence on book purchase by schools, and in proposing and promoting what they regard as adequate levels of expenditure on textbooks and library books. Their information is primarily aimed at the publishing and bookselling markets but is nevertheless useful in a library context.

The expenditure needed at 1992/93 levels to provide each pupil with a good supply of books is proposed by Book Trust in its report *Books in schools* as follows:

	Text books per pupil £	Library books per pupil £	Total books per pupil £
Primary			
Good provision	14.92	6.96	21.88
Reasonable provision	12.37	5.78	18.15
Secondary			
Good provision	23.49	10.98	34.47
Reasonable provision	20.26	9.43	29.69

To achieve the right sort of basic provision of class and library books, Book Trust calculated that schools need to spend about 2% of their annual budget on books, representing about £20 for a primary and £30 for a secondary pupil.[12]

A survey by the Educational Publishers' Council, whose figures relate to expenditure in the financial year 1992/93, found that:

- 78.6% of primary schools spent less than £20 per pupil on books in 1992/93, with 18.1% spending less than £5; 70.2% spent less than the Book Trust recommended 2% of their budgets on books, with 42.5% spending less than 1%;

- 66.5% of secondary schools spent less than £30 per pupil, with 13.9% spending less than £10; 72.4% spent less than 2% of their budgets on books, with 41% of the total spending less than 1%;

- 56.5% of schools regard the adequacy of their book funds as low; 23.8% regard them as entirely inadequate.[13]

Although the provision of books to support the National Curriculum has been accepted as a central government responsibility, expenditure by schools on books continues to be supplemented by input from parent-teacher associations (PTAs) and other non-official sources:

- in the primary sector, 21.1% of schools indicate that over 20% of expenditure on books comes from PTA and other unofficial sources; overall, 40.1% claimed that more than 5% of their book expenditure came from PTA sources;

- in the secondary sector, 10.2% of schools derived more than 5% of their book expenditure from PTA and other unofficial sources, with 2.3% deriving over 20%.

In England and Wales, book purchases to support the introduction of the National Curriculum were included in the categories of programme supported by Grants for Educational Support and Training (GEST) from 1991 to 1993. Since 1993/94, the book purchase category has been subsumed in broader curriculum-related categories. While it can be difficult for a school to say which expenditure was funded from that source, in 1992/93:

- in 55% of primary schools GEST money represented less than 10% of expenditure on books (although 22.1% still drew over 20% from this source);

- 67.5% of secondary schools drew on GEST money for less than 10% of their book expenditure, with only 6.1% drawing more than 20% from this source;

- 73.7% of primary schools and 61.9% of secondary schools favour an element of GEST funding being earmarked for purchase of books.

National Curriculum working parties have stressed the need for new text books if the curriculum is to work as it should. It is clear from the Book Trust and EPC data, not only that spending by schools on both class and library books is inadequate overall but also that there are huge disparities in spending between individual schools.

Given the situation as described, and the apparently unequivocal termination of earmarked GEST funding, **we are concerned that adequate investment in books and library services should be maintained where it has been reached already, or introduced where it has not**. Our concern springs from our view not only that **schools must take the responsibility for providing adequate libraries but also that their failure to do so can have a harmful and unjustifiable impact on the public library service, to say nothing of the pupils**. Although we acknowledge that it is unrealistic to recommend to central government that there should be nationally-prescribed levels of funding, it is clear to us that **local decision-making would be greatly assisted by authoritative guidance on the need for adequate investment in library terms to deliver the National Curriculum**.

4.2.3 Standards and access

The Book Trust and Educational Publishers Council (EPC) data, together with numerous reports by HM Inspectors over the years, point up the huge disparities in standards of book and library provision. These disparities arise as much from the lack of enforceable standards and the differing perceptions on the part of school managers as to the importance of a library, as from inadequate budgets. In a situation where a school cannot even be obliged to provide a library at all, standards of provision are unlikely to be enforceable.

Reports over recent years from HM Inspectors of Schools refer to the emphasis in the National Curriculum on access to, and the skills to use, class and school libraries – for wider reading, for general study and for the development of information-handling skills. A survey of 42 primary schools in various areas of England in 1989-90 drew the conclusion that "those proper demands may often, in the short term, be frustrated".[14] A survey of secondary schools in a metropolitan district in 1988 revealed that "Few of the libraries are currently able adequately to meet pupils' learning, broader reading or leisure needs".[15] In one English county in 1991 it was found that "Only half the schools in this survey have library stocks which are adequately aligned to the curricula taught".[16] The consequence of this is inequality of access: **pupils in far too many schools are being denied the access to relevant and required books (and to the benefits that reading confers) to which they are entitled as part of the educational system.**

In the education sector, inspection procedures were introduced to ensure that standards are maintained and that funding levels to individual institutions are linked to their performance. Inspection is carried out through full-time inspectorates supplemented by part-time inspectors and there are formal measures and criteria against which performance is judged. Libraries in schools are monitored as part of the Department for Education inspection procedures carried out by the Office for Standards in Education (OFSTED).

School inspections carried out under the aegis of OFSTED are inspections of the whole school and aim to evaluate all resources for learning in the school, including libraries and resource centres. As a general rule, levels of provision are not specified in the OFSTED *Handbook for the inspection of schools,*[17] although reliable indicators (if they exist) can be circulated to registered inspectors in advance of inspection. Amendments to the existing *Handbook* in respect of libraries will be influenced by the way in which resource issues feature in the 391 secondary inspection reports expected in the current round.

We are concerned that the inspection procedures lack depth so far as both quantity and quality of library provision is concerned. While we accept that the Department for Education would not wish to prescribe nationally-applicable criteria for use in inspections to judge the adequacy of library provision and use, we believe that the criteria contained in the *Handbook* should be expanded, sharpened and made more explicit, possibly through the inclusion in the *Handbook* of a technical paper on inspecting libraries.

As a starting point, we should like to see quantitative indicators developed for the guidance of Inspectors relating to:

- national and local levels of expenditure against which to make comparisons;

- use of schools library services within use of out-of-school resources;

- specification of numbers and types of learning resources;

- specification of levels of expenditure;

- physical size and facilities of school library.

4.2.4 Education and training of teachers

In an educational setting, the most important influence on young people's choice of, and enthusiasm for, books is the teacher. The Children's Literature Research Centre pilot survey shows that among influences in choosing books to read, librarians — whether at school or in the public library — come well down the list for both boys and girls, particularly in the 4 to 7 and 11 to 16 age groups, and are certainly a lesser influence than parents, friends and teachers. The influence of parents would be expected at an early age, and it is not surprising that the element of independent choice becomes stronger with age and then predominant in the 11 to 16 age group. But the survey finds that a large proportion of 7 to 11 year-olds would like more help in choosing books, and observes that "At this dynamic phase, good choice is crucial to the process of creating enthusiastic readers". But in this crucial phase, only 4.41% of boys and 9.21% of girls ask the school librarian (if they have one) and 10.29% of boys and 11.84% of girls ask the local public librarian, against 47.06% of boys and 36.84% of girls who ask their teachers.[18]

The importance of teachers having knowledge of and enthusiasm for children's literature is clear.

The importance of the school in bringing children and young people into contact with books, and giving them opportunities not only for reading but for book purchase through school bookshops and school-based book clubs, is proven in other local surveys, for example, of 100 boys and girls aged 9 to 10 in three schools in Hampshire.[19]

In an educational setting also, the most important influence on young people's use of the library is often not the librarian, but the teacher. The need for teachers to receive some basic training in library and information skills if they are to pass these on to their pupils, and so encourage and enable them to make full use of the services available through school and public libraries (and, in later life, other types of libraries) has been often argued, but still deserves emphasis. The case was well set out in a Unesco report in 1986[20] and is supported by research funded by the British Library into student teachers' use of library facilities.[21]

Evidence suggests that the whole issue of effective provision, use and management of learning resources is largely ignored at the initial teacher-training stage, as are information handling skills.

The situation will not be helped by current moves towards school-based training which can only reduce initial teacher training students' exposure to good library services. At present most of them enjoy the use of a well-stocked college library, which usually includes an extensive collection of children's books and teaching resources, providing an example of good practice for them to carry into their subsequent work in schools. As the time they spend in college is reduced, so this experience will be diminished.

In these circumstances, **the importance of in-service training (INSET) for teachers which will instil and maintain an awareness of the importance of the library as the foundation of the curriculum, and of the wider resources available through other libraries, and the ability to exploit its resources to the benefit of pupils' reading and information handling skills, cannot be overstated**.

Allied to this, we are concerned at the lack of education and training in school librarianship. At a time when an increasing number of schools, local education authority, grant-maintained and independent, are wishing to appoint qualified librarians to run their libraries (frequently thanks to the influence of the schools library service) there appears to be a dearth of suitably qualified or experienced librarians to match demand. As with children's librarianship (see 4.1.6) there are few courses or modules in school librarianship on offer at British Librarianship and Information Studies (LIS) schools. Since the librarian in a school can be professionally isolated, the scope for in-house training may be restricted. The onus would seem to lie with the LIS schools themselves to develop in-service courses, possibly offered through schools library services, for librarians working in the school sector.

Leeds Metropolitan University
Professional Diploma in School Library Studies
A semi-distance learning course for teachers

University of Central England
In-service Training Courses

Key conclusions

● Adequate investment by schools in books and library services should be maintained where it has been reached already, or introduced where it has not. [4.2.2]

● Schools must take the responsibility for providing adequate libraries; their failure to do so can have a harmful and unjustifiable impact on the public library service, to say nothing of the pupils. [4.2.2]

● Local decision-making would be greatly assisted by authoritative guidance on the need for adequate investment in library terms to deliver the National Curriculum. [4.2.2]

● Pupils in far too many schools are being denied the access to relevant and required books (and to the benefits that reading confers) to which they are entitled as part of the educational system. [4.2.3]

● Inspection procedures lack depth so far as both quantity and quality of library provision in schools is concerned. [4.2.3]

● It is vitally important that teachers should have knowledge of and enthusiasm for children's literature. [4.2.4]

● Evidence suggests that the whole issue of effective provision, use and management of learning resources is largely ignored at the initial teacher-training stage, as are information handling skills. [4.2.4]

● The importance of in-service training (INSET) for teachers which will instil and maintain an awareness of the importance of the library as the foundation of the curriculum, and of the wider resources available through other libraries, and the ability to exploit its resources to the benefit of pupils' reading and information handling skills, cannot be overstated. [4.2.4]

Recommendations

■ The Department for Education should issue guidance which reflects the need for support through books, learning resources and specialist advice to enable schools to deliver the National Curriculum. DFE should ask the Office for Standards in Education and school governing bodies to monitor local provision against this guidance. [4.2.2]

– DFE; OFSTED; School Governing Bodies and Head Teachers

■ The Department for Education and the Department of National Heritage, together with other relevant bodies such as the School Curriculum Assessment Authority, should initiate and co-ordinate work on issues relating to library book provision to support children's learning. DNH should take the lead in this work. [4.2.3]

– DFE; DNH; SCAA

■ The criteria contained in the Office for Standards in Education *Handbook* for use in inspections to judge the adequacy of library provision and use should be expanded, sharpened and made more explicit, possibly through the inclusion of a Technical paper on inspecting libraries in the *Handbook*. [4.2.3]

– OFSTED

■ School governing bodies should have a strategy for meeting the library and information needs of the curriculum, as part of the school's curriculum policy, and should keep this under review through a mechanism such as an annual report or review. [4.2.3]

The strategy should promote teachers' knowledge of children's literature and understanding of information skills, and ensure that there are means through which this can be achieved. There should be co-ordination between librarians and teachers, and in-service training (INSET) for teachers should draw on the specialist skills of librarians in the public library's children's service and the schools library service, as happens already in some schools. [4.2.4]

Schools should introduce children to the public library service. [4.2.4]

– School Governing Bodies and Head Teachers; Library Managers

4.3 Schools library services

4.3.1 Current structures

In England and Wales, schools library services are the responsibility of the counties and metropolitan districts, and the London boroughs; traditionally, the services are operated by the library department of the local authority as an agent of the education department, with costs normally being met from the education budget. There is no statutory obligation on the local education authority to provide such central services in support of school libraries, either directly or through the public library as agency; there is at the time of writing no schools library service in at least one metropolitan district and one county in England, four London boroughs, and two of the counties in Wales.

The anomaly of being administratively in libraries but operationally in education does not exist in Northern Ireland, where the five Education and Library Boards are responsible for both education and library services, and the schools library service is a statutory function; or in Scotland, where schools library services are for the most part provided as a statutory function of the regional education service (the situation in Scotland may change if the proposed reform of local government abolishes the regional authorities).

Schools library services have been subject to fundamental change in recent years resulting from the passing of the Education Reform Act 1988 and the introduction of Local Management of Schools (LMS). Delegation to individual schools of the budget for the schools library service (as part of central services) has affected the funding and operation of the services in England and Wales, and the situation is not only complex but also volatile. Although delegation has actually happened in only a minority of authorities, phased delegation over several years is scheduled to take place by 1994/95 in a far greater number of others; the number of those in which no delegation is foreseen has fallen from 70 in 1991/92 to 35 in 1992/93.[22] Schools with delegated budgets now have to decide whether or not to 'buy back' into the central schools library service for all or some of its services, and their judgement in this must be influenced by the quality of central services on offer and by their cost as well as by the schools' perceived need for library support service at all.

In a growing number of areas, alternative structures for the schools library service have been introduced, such as management by the local education authority, or creation of an independent business unit. The direction that a schools library service takes depends in large measure on the local culture: while nearly half of existing services have formed themselves into business units, and four contemplate complete independence, in 25% of authorities no change has even been discussed.[23] A few services have been dismantled altogether or run down to a minimal level.

4.3.2 Funding

Of 81 authorities reporting budget figures to Library and Information Statistics Unit (LISU) for 1992/93 and 1993/94, 37% show an increase in the current over the previous year, usually of a modest percentage; 6% are at a standstill; 23% show a small decrease equivalent to a tightening of budget with possibly a few schools removing from the service; 33% report a major decrease indicating structural change or reorganisation. Most of the decreases are due to expenditure moving out of the schools library service through delegation of all or part of its budget.

Overall, the average spending as reported has declined. However, materials funds show wide *per capita* variations between different authorities from under £1 per local education authority (LEA) pupil in counties such as Humberside and Kent to over £5 in Berkshire and Northumberland; in metropolitan districts, from less than 50 pence in such as Bury and Salford to over £4 in Stockport; in London, from less than 50 pence in such as Bexley and Haringey to over £3 in Harrow and over £6 in Islington. Total budgets also show wide *per capita* variations. LISU 1992/93 comments that "it is difficult to establish any trend in the schools library service: the figures are down, but comparability with previous years is vitiated by the delegation of budgets".[24]

There seems little doubt that funding overall, and funding priorities within local education authorities and individual schools, will result in a continuing need to balance resources between sustaining existing services and introducing new ones, between meeting existing and future needs. The majority of schools library services now understand the need to operate in a market economy, to sell services in which value can be seen to be added, and to demonstrate the benefits of buying these services.

There is a view that Local Management of Schools has led to the diminution of schools library services through schools deciding not to buy back into central services such as the schools library service. This has led in some parts of the country to the schools library service coming under considerable pressure to maintain its service and standards. The extent of schools buying back into the schools library service is clearly crucial to the latter's survival and its mode of operation. To date, the situation is not without some encouragement. Of 23 authorities where delegation had taken place by 1992/93 (the extent of the budget delegated ranging from 2% to 100%), 12 report buying back at between 90% and 100%; elsewhere, with two exceptions, there is a substantial proportion of buying back.[25]

Individual schools' commitment to buy back schools library services could only be guaranteed if the Department for Education were to earmark funds specifically for this purpose, and for it to introduce some form of oversight or monitoring to ensure that such earmarked funds were properly allocated. We do not see this as a realistic scenario. **We do, however, envisage that the guidance for schools on adequate investment in school libraries, recommended at 4.2.2 and 4.2.6,**

should incorporate advice on the need to support these libraries by buying services from the schools library service.

4.3.3 Factors conditioning ability to meet needs

Many of the factors that condition the ability of schools library services to meet needs arise out of the current situation as outlined in 4.3.1 with regard to delegation of budgets and willingness of schools to buy back on a scale sufficient to ensure not only the financial viability of the service but also its continuing ability to maintain a scale of operation that will allow specialised services to be maintained. There are also other factors arising from the local authority context in which schools library services operate, both in its traditional *modus operandi* and its possible future structure, and from recent legislation, with its potential for differing interpretation.

Funding

Local management of schools and the extent of individual schools' purchase of services is clearly critical to the future shape and nature of schools library services.

Local government financial procedures

The existing local government context imposes regulations, financial cut-offs, etc, instead of the kind of climate that real businesses need to prosper and expand: venture capital, overdraft facilities, development funds to finance new ventures. These restrictions have the potential to affect the operation of services that establish themselves as business units.

Local government reform

While the outcome of the local government review has fundamental implications for county library and education services in general, the potential replacement of a county unit by a number of smaller unitary authorities raises particular concerns among schools library services, concerns which have been increasingly urgently expressed during the period of the Working Party's life. Although there are as yet few firm proposals for English counties, there is no doubt that schools library services in general regard local government reform as a major threat to the quality of service provided to schools and, not impossibly, to their continued existence.

The concern of the schools library services themselves centres on the loss of the economy of scale permitted by a county-wide enterprise which allows the critical mass of specialist staffing and resources which alone can give schools the value-added service which distinguishes their unique role in educational support. British Library-funded research by Midwinter and McVicar into the relationship between population size and functional efficiency in public library authorities, based on the evidence of Chartered Institute of Public Finance and Accountancy statistics, while acknowledging that "size is not the only factor determining the scope and range of services", does confirm some "diseconomies of scale in small library authorities, which incur greater expenditure per 1,000 population than larger authorities, and require more facilities to provide the service".[26]

In Somerset, it is proposed that the county be replaced by three unitary authorities of unequal size and with very different numbers of schools within each. Estimates of the cost implications of each of the new services offering the same level of provision per user as the present county service Resources 4 Learning, are that 11.3 extra staff from service manager/senior librarian to drivers would be required (incurring not only basic salary and on-costs but also costs of relocation, recruitment, severance, and training for induction and reskilling) and that the additional lending stock costs would be in the order of £416,000 plus costs of reprocessing. Additional costs would be incurred on bibliographical support, accommodation, vehicles, equipment and furniture, stationery and printing, and administration and central support. Precise costs obviously cannot be given in the Somerset statement of implications, but the order of magnitude is apparent.[27]

From evidence such as this throughout the country, the Coopers & Lybrand report concludes that:

> "Local governmment reorganisation is likely to have a major impact on the SLS [schools library services] in county areas. If current arrangements are fragmented the likelihood of this being to the detriment of services and schools is strong with a consequent loss of economies of scale, specialist expertise and breadth of service. There are alternatives to fragmentation but these involve as yet untried consortia or externalisation approaches and are not without their potential disadvantages."[28]

Restrictions on trading

Schools library services, like all local authority services, are subject to restrictions on trading. There are three principal restrictions, one which can arise from local council policy and two from current legislation:

- council policy may prevent the schools library service from trading with grant-maintained or independent schools within its area;
- the Local Authorities (Goods and Services) Act 1970 permits a schools library service (as part of the local education authority) to provide goods and services to other local authorities and to grant-maintained schools within its own area, but only within its 'margins of capacity', ie, as a spin-off from what it provides as part of its primary function;
- Section 295 of the Education Act 1993 allows the sale of services to grant-maintained schools but only for a period of two years from the point in time when the service has reached the margins of its capacity. Beyond the two-year period, it is expected that private sector suppliers will have moved into the market (a notion that is strongly challenged by the Coopers & Lybrand study).[29]

The problem for schools library services in trying to plan their future is the varying interpretations of these restrictive measures. Limitations on trading with grant-maintained schools could seriously undermine the viability of the customer base for a schools library service in a county with a high proportion of such schools; limitations on cross-border trading are perhaps less serious in the short term but in the longer term could be counter-productive for both suppliers and potential customers. Advice on the legislative aspects comes from both the Department of Environment and the Department for Education, and may not coincide with the interpretations of local district auditors or the policies of councils. We believe that **there is a need for clarification and authoritative guidance (not subject to local interpretation) on the issue of trading 'at the margins' and 'beyond capacity' that will enable schools library services to see their way forward as business ventures**.

Key conclusions

● Guidance for schools on adequate investment in school libraries, discussed at 4.2.2, should emphasise the need to support the school library (whatever its level of investment) through buying back specialist services from the schools library service. [4.3.2]

● There is a need for clarification and authoritative guidance (not subject to local interpretation) on the issue of trading 'at the margins' and 'beyond capacity' that will enable schools library services to see their way forward as business ventures. [4.3.3]

Recommendations

There are no recommendations specifically relating to schools library services. As one of the three principal channels of service delivery to children and young people, they are included in the integrated strategy proposed in Recommendation 1.

4.4   Information base

In formulating a view on the current situation, the importance of regular and reliable comprehensive statistical information to inform debate has to be emphasised. Public library services to children aged 0 to 14, and schools library services, are well covered; but there is a lack of comparable statistical information on school libraries, and further education college libraries. A firm statistical base is vital: as evidence of service, as exemplar of differences both local and national, and inter-sectoral, and to point up gaps and weaknesses so that they can be remedied.

4.4.1 Public library services for children and young people

Services for children and young people in public libraries are covered annually by the statistical volume *A survey of library services to schools and children in the UK* published by the Library and Information Statistics Unit (LISU), the most recent figures available at the time of writing being for the financial year 1992/93. The Working Party has also had available to it a wealth of information contributed as part of its summer 1993 data collection exercise by county and metropolitan district libraries in England and county and district libraries in Wales.

There has been no full-scale research into children's services in public libraries since Edmonds and Miller *Public library services for children and young people: a statistical survey*, the report of a British Library-funded survey of all 108 English authorities covering the years 1982/83 to 1986/87, which forms the precursor to the LISU annual surveys.[30]

4.4.2 School libraries

Statements on this sector are handicapped by the absence of reliable comprehensive statistical information such as exists for public libraries and for schools library services. "The inevitable conclusion to be drawn by anybody investigating statistics about school libraries is that there is a real need for a comprehensive national survey which would provide some much needed hard information about what is at the moment statistically uncharted territory."[31] However, a national survey, unless statutorily enforced, is unlikely to achieve a comprehensive picture: anything over 10% response would be regarded as good, and statistically reliable.

The most recent survey of school book buying, carried out in 1993 by the Educational Publishers Council (EPC) achieved a response of 10.5%, representing returns from 3,312 out of a possible 31,454 primary and secondary schools throughout the United Kingdom. This forms the most comprehensive and up-to-date body of data at present available, though it is angled to book purchase in general rather than libraries in particular, being intended to "provide information on book spending in schools which can be used by EPC in its campaigning material to encourage schools to spend a reasonable amount of their budget on books; specifically it needs to provide an average bench mark on what is being spent at present in order to set it against the recommended Book Trust figures for 'good' and 'reasonable' provision for primary and secondary schools"[32] (see 4.2.2).

The other major source of information is the Office for Standards in Education. Plans to inspect 25% of schools every year mean that information collected in the course of inspections will form a continuing database. If OFSTED were able to collect expenditure statistics in as much detail as possible for books and learning materials, and if an agreed structure for continuing collection and dissemination could be agreed, the OFSTED school inspection cycle could provide a more viable and cost-effective vehicle than specially-mounted surveys. In any case, **we would urge the need for early publication of the data being collected by OFSTED with a view to ascertaining its usefulness and, if necessary, encouraging the fuller and more targeted collection of information**.

4.4.3 Schools library services

Schools library services are comprehensively covered by the statistical information collected by LISU and published annually as *A survey of library services to schools and children in the UK*. The current volume, covering 1992/93, achieved an overall response rate of 94%. With regard to schools library services, the comparability of information between individual authorities and between types of authority has been affected by factors such as the delegation of budgets to schools under LMS, changes in the demarcation between libraries and education, schools buying back from the schools library service, merging of schools library services into education departments (as opposed to libraries). Nevertheless, the current volume can be regarded as presenting a picture that is close to reality in most respects, and certainly informs the issues for discussion.

Key conclusions

● A firm statistical base is vital: as evidence of service, as exemplar of differences both local and national, and inter-sectoral, and to point up gaps and weaknesses so that they can be remedied. [4.4]

● Existing and planned data collection by individual bodies should be co-ordinated wherever possible so that mutual benefits for collectors and users can be derived. [4.4]

• We would urge the need for early publication of the data being collected by the Office for Standards in Education with a view to ascertaining its usefulness and, if necessary, encouraging the fuller and more targeted collection of information. [4.4.2]

Recommendation

■ Adequate statistical information must be produced, and trends monitored, to establish a comprehensive national picture of services and levels of provision, and to identify disparities in standards of service in order to facilitate local decision-making. [4.4]

Co-ordination of data gathering between agencies that already collect data on library services and book provision for children should be investigated, and effected if feasible. [4.4]

– LISU; CIPFA; OFSTED; LA and its specialist groups; Book Trust; EPC

References

1. ASLIB CONSULTANCY. *DNH review of the public library service in England and Wales: draft report, September 1994.* The Aslib Consultancy, 1994.
2. NATIONAL BOOK COMMITTEE. *Public libraries and their book funds.* Book Trust, 1993.
3. LIBRARY AND INFORMATION STATISTICS UNIT. *A survey of library services to schools and children in the UK* 1992-93 by Helen Pickering and John Sumsion. Loughborough University of Technology, LISU, 1993.
4. ASLIB CONSULTANCY. *DNH review of the public library service in England and Wales: preliminary information, August 1994.* Aslib, 1994.
5. LIBRARY AND INFORMATION STATISTICS UNIT *op. cit.*
6. DEPARTMENT OF NATIONAL HERITAGE. *Library and information provision in rural areas of England and Wales: a report by Capital Planning Information Ltd.* HMSO, 1993. Library information series no.20.
7. LIBRARY AND INFORMATION STATISTICS UNIT *op. cit.*
8. LIBRARY ASSOCIATION. *Children and young people: Library Association guidelines for public library services.* Library Association Publishing Ltd, 1991.
9. ASLIB CONSULTANCY, *op. cit.*
10. DEPARTMENT OF NATIONAL HERITAGE. *Schools library services and financial delegation to schools* [report by Coopers & Lybrand] Draft, 1994.
11. CHILDREN'S LITERATURE RESEARCH CENTRE. *Contemporary juvenile reading habits: a study of young people's reading at the end of the century.* Roehampton Institute, CLRC, 1994.
12. BOOK TRUST. *Books in schools.* Book Trust, 1992. Book Trust Report 1, British National Bibliography Research Fund Report 60.
13. EDUCATIONAL PUBLISHERS' COUNCIL. *School book buying survey 1992-93: a report on data gathered directly from the schools;* prepared by Trevor Osbourn and Roger Watson. EPC, 1993.

14. DEPARTMENT OF EDUCATION AND SCIENCE. *Library provision and use in 42 primary schools September 1989 – July 1990: a report by HMI.* DES, 1991.

15. DEPARTMENT OF EDUCATION AND SCIENCE. *A survey of libraries in 12 secondary schools in Barnsley: report by HM Inspectors.* DES, 1989.

16. DEPARTMENT OF EDUCATION AND SCIENCE. *A survey of library provision and use in ten Lancashire secondary schools: a report by HMI.* DES, 1991.

17. OFFICE FOR STANDARDS IN EDUCATION. *Handbook for the inspection of schools;* May 1994 amendment. HMSO, 1994.

18. CHILDREN'S LITERATURE RESEARCH CENTRE *op. cit.*

19. Survey carried out by a head teacher in Hampshire and reported via the School Library Association submission.

20. HALL, N. *Teachers, information and school libraries.* Paris, Unesco, 1986.

21. BEST, RE, ABBOTT, F and TAYLOR, M. *Teaching skills for learning: information skills in initial teacher education.* British Library, 1990. Library and information research report 78.

22. LIBRARY AND INFORMATION STATISTICS UNIT *op. cit.*

23. BOYD, Rachel. *The future for school library services.* Paper to the School Libraries Group Weekend School, 18 April 1993.

24. LIBRARY AND INFORMATION STATISTICS UNIT *op. cit.*

25. LIBRARY AND INFORMATION STATISTICS UNIT *op. cit.*

26. MIDWINTER, Arthur and McVICAR, Murray. Population size and functional efficiency in public library authorities: the statistical evidence. *Journal of Librarianship and Information Science* 25(4) December 1993, 187-196.

27. RESOURCES 4 LEARNING. *Cost implications of setting up three distinct services in new unitary authorities.* Unpublished paper, 1994.

28. DEPARTMENT OF NATIONAL HERITAGE. *Schools library services and financial delegation to schools* [report by Coopers & Lybrand] Draft, 1994.

29. DEPARTMENT OF NATIONAL HERITAGE, *op. cit.*

30. EDMONDS, Diana and MILLER, Jane. *Public library services for children and young people: a statistical survey.* British Library, 1990. Library and information research report 72.

31. MARRIOTT, Richard. *School and college library statistics.* In LISU Information policy briefing no.3, 8 June 1993.

32. EDUCATIONAL PUBLISHERS' COUNCIL *op. cit.*

5 Libraries meeting needs: the way forward

5.1 Factors for the future

Our main focus has been the role of the public library in meeting the child's need for books and information. The concern is to establish children and young people as a distinct and recognised client group. The group is not characterised by its homogeneity: within it, there are a range of client groups having differing needs according to age and stage of development. It is, however, a client group whose special needs require special provision as part of the core of the public library service.

Since the child's need is for a total service that provides books and other material through appropriate channels and in appropriate places, we have also taken into account library services provided by those responsible for educational spending – school libraries and the centralised schools library services – and considered their relationships with, and impact on, the public library service.

In considering the way forward, there are factors which can be construed as being unhelpful to effective provision:

- Local management of schools (LMS) has fragmented budgetary responsibility for school libraries and for schools library services.

- Competitive tendering in the public sector has introduced the prospect of public library services, including perhaps children's services, being contracted out and run by private sector companies, introducing the principle of profitability and thereby the prospect of charges for some services.

- The trend towards generalist management in local government is leading to a reduction in specialist posts at senior management level.

- Library and information schools have reduced their courses in children's and school librarianship, largely as a result of their perception of a dwindling market for specialists in the public sector, but leading to greatly reduced numbers of trained staff for public and education libraries. This places a heavy emphasis on in-service training.

- Local government reform will break up a number of English county authorities leading to the dismemberment of county library resources and services and of schools library services, and to the delegation of responsibility for public library provision to a greater number of smaller authorities which may not have the resources to provide a 'comprehensive and efficient service' and may therefore need to make other arrangements. Whether they have the resources or not, the **responsibility** will remain.

These factors cannot be avoided, even though they may not be universally acceptable. They can and they do cause difficulties, but they represent the changed and changing environment in which libraries must seek constructive solutions and strategies to meet the needs of their young customers.

There are many examples from many parts of the UK of libraries of all kinds which despite, and sometimes because of, problems and constraints, have maintained the excellence of their services by one means or another, and which have seen in a changed environment opportunities for imaginative developments in service delivery. While shortage of resources can preclude the achievement of full potential, there is nevertheless sufficient positive achievement to provide a basis on which future services can build.

Some of these developments are highlighted in the text. They are not promoted as 'exceptional practice' (for what is good in one area may not be good for another) but as examples of service initiatives from which any library can take heart and inspiration in planning for an uncertain future.

5.2   Strategy for service delivery

The public library's primary responsibility is to provide books and other material to satisfy the recreational, educational, cultural and information needs of all members of the population, including children and young people. Education has always been regarded as one of the fundamental roles of the public library and a central focus of library provision for children and young people, whose principal need between the ages of 5 and 16 is in support of their formal education.

The public library, however, is not intended to provide formal support for the teaching of the National Curriculum in schools. Formal support is primarily the responsibility of the schools themselves. Many schools do provide class books for in-school use and for homework purposes, and do provide libraries for both school and wider educational and recreational purposes, within the limits of their available budgets and in accord with the priority attached to such provision. Schools library services are there to support the school in a wide range of areas including supply of learning resources, expertise, advice and liaison. Beyond this, the public library is available to all individuals (as institutional libraries can not be) who need its resources for school-related or for broader educational purposes.

That library provision is falling short of necessary levels in some schools is borne out by the statistics presented in Section 4.2.2, and it is clear that where schools are providing less than adequate services either through inadequate library provision or through failure to buy into the schools library service, the public library is generally regarded as at least a backstop and at most a substitute.

The public library service in general is not adequately resourced to make up for the deficiencies of educational institutions that can not or will not provide sufficient textbooks and library books for their own pupils, nor does it have professional specialist staff in sufficient numbers to cope with the additional demands from pupils who are often inadequately briefed by teachers and unable to use books and other information sources for themselves. It has become clear to us that the short-term/high-volume demands arising from the National Curriculum have placed public library services under considerable strain at a time when their budgets are under pressure and demands on them from many client groups have increased. Eventually, the impact on public libraries should lessen following the recent review and revision of the National

Curriculum in accord with the lessening of specific demand within the Attainment Targets, but at this stage it is impossible to predict the actual outcome.

The challenge facing libraries today is that the changing cultures and environment noted in 5.1, as well as introducing challenges and opportunities, have also given rise to compartmentalisation, and to fragmentation of relationships and delivery of services. Previously, roles, functions and relationships between the principal channels were defined to varying degrees of precision, and some overlapping of functions was accepted in the interests of the child. Some cross-sectoral activity was regarded as beneficial to children and young people by sustaining and developing the library habit in a holistic way.

This changed, and changing, environment has tended to push the principal library channels apart rather than bring them together. Within this context, there are undoubtedly problems for libraries of all types in meeting the needs of children and young people. Problems of access to public libraries, caused by rationalisation or reduction in the network of service points and changes in opening hours of the service points, present particular difficulties for children, who may then be doubly disadvantaged through reduction in education library services.

Against this background, **we are convinced that an integrated strategy for delivery of library services for children and young people through individual school libraries, the schools library service, and the public library, is necessary to support the needs of the National Curriculum, and broader educational needs both in and out of school**. Within this totality of library services for children and young people, it is necessary to be absolutely clear about the roles and relationships of the players on the scene. Ultimately a library is responsible to the source of its funding and is governed by its rules; equally, each body is responsible for its own library service and must accept that responsibility. Responsibility can be more easily accepted if the role is defined. Similarly, roles can be more easily defined if the necessary relationships with other providers are known and understood and if the extent of inter-dependence is clear.

We also believe that such **an integrated strategy should be devised and owned by the local authority and its components and agencies to meet the needs of its local community of children**. The local education authority, while it has no statutory requirement to provide school library facilities, has a strategic responsibility for the provision of education within its area. This responsibility should include production of an integrated strategy within which responsibility for each element of delivery is assigned and accepted, and inter-relationships between them made clear. The strategy would provide for the support of the National Curriculum through adequate library services in schools, supported by schools library services, and complemented by proper liaison between public libraries and teachers in schools and between schools library services and both of these.

We have been greatly concerned to find that there is little evidence of a response such as we have outlined: we have experienced considerable difficulty in identifying examples of integrated strategies at local level. Although none of the examples referred to below embrace the fully integrated strategy led by the local education authority that we believe to be the best possible solution, that of North Tyneside in particular represents a genuine policy of integration to provide a total library service for children and young people, while some partial responses can be seen in the service level agreements between a public library and a schools library service in the same area, or between a schools library service and the schools that it serves.

North Tyneside Libraries
Children and Young People's Library Service

Cambridgeshire County Council
Public Library Services to Schools:
Service Level Agreement with Schools Library Service
*This spells out what public libraries **will** provide
and what they **will not** provide*

Northumberland Schools Library Service
Service Level Agreements

Along with the lack of evidence of integrated policies at local level, we have found at national level an absence of the integration of approach and clear view of the place of libraries in support of education that would encourage integration at local level. Parliamentary debates on school libraries and the schools library service during the passage of the 1993 Education Act have shown the division of responsibility between the Department of National Heritage and the Department for Education to be unhelpful. Where liaison and good relationships exist at present, they are dependent upon individuals; there are no formal strategies for co-operation.

We are convinced of the need for co-ordination at national level, and we see the new Library and Information Commission to be set up from January 1995 as providing a vehicle for an integrated approach to the resolution of problems involving libraries in the public and the education sectors, and for formal reconciliation of policies and strategies for libraries of all types to combine in support of education programmes for children and young people.

The Library and Information Commission should have a major concern for the needs of this group, on whose development as readers and as library users depends the future of reading and the proper and cost-effective use of the country's library resources in general.

US National Commission on Libraries and Information Science
A permanent independent federal agency advising Congress and President on library and information matters, and pursuing initiatives regarding the federal role in support of library and information services and literacy programmes for children

---

5.3   The role of the public library

The Public Libraries and Museums Act 1964 places on a local library authority in England and Wales a requirement to address the needs of children as individuals:

> In fulfilling its duty [to provide a comprehensive and efficient library service] a library authority shall in particular have regard to the desirability ...
>
> (a) of securing ... that facilities are available ... sufficient in number, range and quality to meet the general requirements and any special requirements **both of adults and children**; and
>
> (b) of encouraging **both adults and children** to make full use of the library service ...

This statutory responsibility should be emphasised. The Advisory Council on Public Libraries which will, following establishment of the Library and Information Commission, replace the Library and Information Services Council (England) as the advisory body to the Secretary of State for National Heritage on his specific responsibilities for public libraries in England, should ensure that the library needs of children and young people are adequately represented in its deliberations.

The role of the public library in meeting the needs of children and young people is of paramount importance to the future economic and cultural health of this country. Continuation of its service to them, untrammelled by barriers to access such as charging, is a critical factor in the future development of the public library service as a whole.

We find it highly significant that among the preliminary findings of the project team commissioned by the Department of National Heritage to review the public library service in England and Wales is solid confirmation of its role in relation to children and young people. "Enlightening children on the benefits of reading and information discovery" is regarded by three-quarters of sampled users and non-users as one of the two top-ranking functions of the public library, and firmly in the 'core' of its service.[1] "It is a role which fits in well with the purpose many people see for the public library, that is, to serve the interests of future generations."[2]

5.3.1   Charter for children

What children should be entitled to from a core service should be spelled out in a charter specifically relating to children. We regard the following as integral parts of a core service for children:

- provision of appropriate stock;
- access after school as well as during the day;
- homework space;
- availability of trained specialist staff;
- promotion that emphasises the benefits of the library and takes its service to **every** child in its area, irrespective of age, background and culture.

Many public libraries now have charters that formalise what the expectations of their users should be. The Charter for the Reader published by the International Publishers Association and adopted on 28 September 1992 by the International

Book Committee is a good model for general use. The Library Association has also launched a model charter, to which model standards are to be linked (see also 5.3.3).

Few libraries, however, have published charters specifically aimed at children or young people, although a few have agreed that one should be prepared and more see it as an issue that should be addressed. We hope that future versions of the Library Association's charter will expand on the two statements relating to children that the model at present contains:

> 5.3 "We will provide ... special facilities for children";

> 10.2 "We will organise activities for children to encourage them to use the library and to read regularly".

And that the Association will address this issue more fully, taking into account proposals already made by the Youth Libraries Group, and the Association's own campaign 'Library Power' which will be launched in 1995 with the aim of highlighting children's entitlement to proper library services to support their education and development.

South Eastern Education and Library Board, Northern Ireland
'Our Promise to Children'

London Borough of Bromley
'The Child as Customer' in preparation

5.3.2 Aims and objectives

The aims and objectives of the service for children and young people are closely linked to the child's entitlement to service as described in a Charter. Essentially, the Charter states what the customer should expect of the library; the aims and objectives state what the library hopes to do to meet these expectations.

Nottinghamshire County Library Service
Public Library Services to Children:
Aims, Objectives and Performance Indicators

As we said at the beginning of Section 2 (and we do not hesitate to repeat it here) we believe that the needs of children and young people for books, for libraries and for encouragement of reading and the use of information, should be the starting point for any consideration of library services delivered to them, and that recognition of these needs should inform and determine the aims and objectives of all libraries that serve this client group. This is one of the key conclusions of Section 2.

The needs of children and young people vary widely between different age groups and stages of development, and can be affected by a range of factors. **At a time of**

continuing pressure on resources, a library has to identify its priorities within these needs and to endeavour to meet them through its aims and objectives. The importance of the public library is to ensure that the reading habit is developed at an early age and is maintained into and beyond the teenage years.

It is our view also that **objectives for children's services should reflect the integral part that promotion and outreach play in service delivery**. The library has to go out into the community to reach children, and their parents and carers, and should be ready to use non-traditional means of achieving this (see also 5.6.1).

5.3.3 Standards

Apart from Scotland, where standards for the public library service were published in 1987, and are currently being revised by the Convention of Scottish Local Authorities (COSLA) there are no published national standards to which the expectations expressed in a charter can be linked. In the current climate of financial restraint and uncertainty, and of differing local cultures, **we cannot see the imposition of national standards as a realistic goal**.

We refute the popular proposition that standards are exclusively related to funding levels. While the ability to meet 'high' standards of service provision does rely on adequate funding, nevertheless, even within levels of funding that are perceived as being low, standards of quality and levels of service can and should be set, and met.

It is increasingly the case that the standards of service expected in an individual public library are expressed in the form of service specifications (particularly where contracting out is envisaged, or a reality, or where the service is established on a client/contractor basis) and service level agreements.

Berkshire Department of Libraries, Archives and Tourism
Specification for Children's Services in Public Libraries
Covers customers, core service, stock, staffing, accommodation, and promotion, with performance indicators for each

Birmingham Library Services (Community Services)
Service Level Agreement with the Children, Youth and Education Team

---

We would not disagree with this practice so long as local standards are made explicit, and can be related to the rightful expectations of the customer as stated in the charter. Our view is that the actual standards achieved by individual local authorities should be declared and made known through a watching brief by the Department of National Heritage as an explicit part of its existing superintending role.

Guidance to what can be achieved locally is more realistically provided through benchmarks of good or innovative service to which others can aspire (see Appendix C to this report) and through guidelines such as those published by the Library Association for public library services for children and young people.[3]

In this context, **we endorse the Library Association's current project to develop model standards for public libraries in its aim of producing helpful professional guidance which will be adapted for use locally. It is hoped that some explicit statements may be made regarding the importance of services for children and young people as a core element in the public library's function.**

5.3.4 Quality assessment and performance measurement

Judgements on the quality of a library service are made locally, based on locally-derived standards or guidelines, and using locally-derived performance measures and assessment procedures. We believe that the specification of service underpinned by quality standards are crucial to the future development of services for young people.

Kent Arts and Libraries
Quality Standards

Norfolk Library and Information Service
Quality Statements

Whether standards or guidelines are applied locally, with or without guidance from nationally-conceived models, the quality of the individual library's performance has to be measured against the statements of the charter and the aims and objectives for the children's service. The concept of quality inspection of libraries (analogous to schools inspection) is still evolving, in conjunction with client/contractor situations in which a quality inspection client team monitors the contracted out libraries.

Westminster Libraries
Quality Inspection Schedule

More common is the use of performance indicators against which the performance of individual libraries can be monitored. Here again, **centrally conceived manuals of performance indicators are unlikely to gain general acceptability**: it is the local measures as expressed in service level agreements and service specifications that will be observed. However, we are of the opinion that **there should be some guidance on performance indicators at national level which can be adapted for use locally as required**. Our view is that performance indicators inform future planning and policy framing and, if promoted and used, can provide a framework for comparison of services.

We have found very few public libraries whose indicators refer explicitly to children's services, although some include children in their categorisation for indicators such as annual issues or book stock. Indicators for children's services do not figure on the Audit Commission's statutory list; its voluntary (recommended) indicators include only one: "Children's book issues per capita". In 1992, John Sumsion observed that "for most authorities, this would be a new indicator, although survey research results have been published for several years by the Library and Information Statistics Unit (LISU) and the British Library. The data on issues is already supplied to the Chartered Institute of Public Finance and Accountancy (CIPFA) by all but a handful of authorities. The population data can be obtained from census figures." Sumsion went on to comment that "There is already pressure to ensure that children escape as far as possible the effects of budget cuts... Publishing the results should tighten performance in particular authorities."[4]

We also take the view that market research in the form of regular user surveys, carried out to professional standards, and covering children as well as parents and carers, is an essential tool in the management of any organisation that serves the public, and provides the firm and unbiased information on which specifications, services and performance management can be evaluated and adjusted in order to meet the needs of customers (see also 4.1.8).

In these connections, we have noted the work of a sub-group of the CIPFA Statistical Information Service's Public Libraries Working Group in developing a national standard in the form of a consistent set of core questions to be used by public libraries when undertaking user surveys. It is expected that these questions, having been agreed following a consultation process, will be administered nationwide on a voluntary basis in 1995/96. The aim of the standard survey is to provide a quality indicator for public libraries. It is not its aim to lay down all the questions that libraries might ask of all their client groups.

The CIPFA sub-group has given considerable thought to the matter of surveying children, bearing in mind that they represent some 20% of public library business, but in view of the difficulties involved in the process, such as the impossibility of administering a single set of questions to adults and children and the need to obtain parents' permission before questioning children below the age of 14, it decided that its standard survey questions cannot at this stage be applied to children.

It is, however, seeking authoritative guidance on the matter from research currently being formulated by the research consortium Childlib (the librarianship and information studies departments of Loughborough University, University of Wales Aberystwyth, and University of Central England) which, within its wide-ranging project aims, expects to identify a methodology for surveying children and young people up to the age of 16 that will tie in with performance indicators for public libraries and their requirements for surveying children in their own local areas. It is hoped that the results of the research will resolve the difficulties encountered by the sub-group as noted above, although it is not anticipated that children could be included in the national survey until 1996/97 at the earliest.

The Library and Information Services Council Working Party endorses the need for the research proposed by the Childlib consortium. **We believe that a proper survey methodology, capable of being applied nationally, is critical to any understanding of the extent to which public libraries are meeting the needs of children and young people**. We wish to associate our own Recommendation 16 together with our comments and conclusions on the matter (3.5, 4.1.8, and above) with the specification and implementation of the research.

5.4 The role of the school library

Ten years ago, the Library and Information Services Council (LISC) published a report *School libraries: the foundations of the curriculum* which has been regarded as a seminal statement on the subject. Its major recommendation to local authorities was "to clarify the objectives of school libraries and the school library service and to establish a policy framework for them".[5] **We believe that the majority of the recommendations of the LISC report on school libraries remain valid in broad terms**. There are a number of specific recommendations arising from that report which we would particularly urge to have re-examined by the bodies to which they were addressed and that efforts be made to ensure that they are implemented. These specific recommendations are set out, in an up-dated form of words, in Appendix D.

Drawing on our observations in 4.2.2 and 4.2.3, together with those of 5.2, we take the view that **there should be a requirement upon schools to demonstrate how they will provide adequate learning resources to underpin the teaching of the National Curriculum, taking into account the support to be drawn from the schools library service and the benefits to be derived from liaison with the public library**. The school's strategy for meeting the library and information needs of the curriculum is seen as being firmly placed within our recommendation for an authority-wide integrated strategy for delivering library service to meet the identified needs of children and young people.

We acknowledge the problem in determining what may be regarded as 'adequate' for each school's individual circumstances. The proportion of each school's delegated budget spent on books and other learning resources is at the discretion of the head teacher and the governing body; central government is unwilling to determine levels of expenditure; and the level of expenditure required will vary from school to school and will in turn depend on the levels of their book stocks and the availability to them of other library services. Some consensus as to adequacy in library terms may emerge from Office for Standards in Education inspections, supported by its new research into the benefits accruing to schools from learning resource provision, but **we cannot see such a consensus emerging unless the criteria contained in the Office for Standards in Education (OFSTED) *Handbook*[6] for use in inspections are expanded, sharpened, and made more explicit**.

Adequacy in provision of learning resources is determined not only by funding but by the way in which the resources are exploited for the benefit of pupils. A key factor in this is the recognition that the **school library is an integral part of curriculum planning for reading and information handling throughout the whole school**. It is clear from the various national awards made to school libraries by such as the National Curriculum Development Council, the Paul Hamlyn Foundation and the Pan Macmillan school library awards, that the active development of a library as an integral part of the curriculum is the main criterion of success in meeting needs.

5.4.1 Information skills

Literacy includes not only the ability to read but also the ability to search for, assemble and present information. Librarians find that many young people do not know how to use information books properly. This is borne out by the Children's Literature Research Centre's pilot study which reports that "a surprisingly high percentage (particularly of boys) still think it is necessary to read every word of an information book rather than use an index … it seems likely that many of them [young people] have yet to develop systematic ways of using them [books] … schools need to be more alert to the need to teach the required kind of strategies".[7]

Information skills "are concerned with the ability to trace sources of information and to extract, arrange and suitably present from these whatever is appropriate to a particular task or need".[8] **The school library, particularly in the secondary school, is the natural base for the teaching of information skills** involving the use of books, of CD-Roms, and of computer databases both in-house and remote. There is evidence that in too many schools, the teaching of these essential information skills has only marginal importance, and that where there is effective teaching it results from the enthusiasm of one or two individuals.

We would echo the view of HM Inspectors of Schools in Scotland that "a library or resource centre focus for a whole school programme of study and information skills is perhaps the very best way to ensure that there is a good return on the finance invested in the library and its curriculum-linked materials".[9] This, in turn, reinforced the view expressed in the 1984 LISC report on school libraries that a school should have a whole school curriculum policy on information skills, underlying all other aspects of curriculum planning.

St Aidan's High School, Wishaw, Scotland
Information Skills Programme

Clwyd Library and Information Service
School Library and Information Skill Development Project

A central part of the teaching of information skills within the curriculum should be recognition of the role of the public library and the resources it has to offer. The public library is, and must be recognised as, the gateway to the full range of public library services and to books and information produced and stored throughout the world. It is also the repository, in its professional librarians, of a considerable expertise in information handling which can be drawn on and used, through the medium of the schools library service, in the development of in-service training (INSET) for teachers.

North Tyneside Libraries
INSET for Teachers

Bolton Libraries, Arts and Archives
Local Studies Training Day

5.5 The role of the schools library service

The crux of the discussion of schools library services is not solely one of funding, but of service orientation and integration with other agencies providing books and library services for children and young people. As a central service agency, not normally in direct contact with children at school, it is a question of role rather than standards or access for individual users. The needs that have to be met now are those of schools as perceived by their teachers and governors, perceptions which are undoubtedly influenced by the exigencies of balancing budgets and weighing priorities among a range of *desiderata*. Schools may decide that their money is better spent on purchasing actual books than on support services; direct selling to schools by educational publishers may be a persuasive factor in this. For their part, schools library services have to convince the schools that what they can offer is the knowledge of books and the expertise in handling them that schools can rarely provide for themselves, and that these things are worth buying.

There is evidence that many schools library services are doing just that. Significant numbers have restructured and revamped services, prepared business plans, revised image and publicity, and other measures to fit their new role of businesses selling services to customers. In some cases, service level agreements have been drawn up, services being decided on the basis of what the customer wants, often following market research. The most recent statistics of schools buying back are encouraging (see 4.3.2) although there are instances of local council policy preventing services from selling to independent or grant-maintained schools in their area; and tighter control of operations is reflected in the almost universal application of performance measures to the most important core activities of stock, issues, school visits and advisory service, while quantitative reports on requests, training and expenditure are also very common.

There is some confidence among schools library services staff that their services will survive, but in a more focused or streamlined form that can readily adapt to change. On the other hand, there is a view that there will be even less equality of access and that service to small schools in particular may suffer, through individual schools' inability to pay for services. The dominant theme is the need to raise awareness of the value of schools library services and the implications of their disappearance both for schools and their pupils, and for the public library service.

We believe most strongly that the future of schools library services must be safeguarded: the impact on school libraries, and on the public library service, should existing services be run down would be immensely damaging. However, given the trend (albeit gradual) towards their integration with education departments rather than with public libraries, and with the impending break-up of a number of English county authorities and Scottish regional authorities as a result of local government reform, we are not convinced that it is realistic to continue to press for statutory status for schools library services (as many have been doing for years) particularly in an environment which favours enablement rather than statutory obligation.

The British Library-funded Supports to Learning Project, reporting in 1992, found that closer links were being forged between schools library services and education services (this is supported by the most recent statistics from the Library and Information Statistics Unit although the trend is not overwhelming) and that there was the beginning of a trend in public libraries towards separation of services to children and services to schools, sometimes without a single professional in charge of both, although again this trend is not overwhelming[10] (see also 4.1.5). The prospect exists that schools library services may eventually be completely separate from the public library service, and may indeed become independent of the local authority altogether.

We referred above (5.4) to the Library and Information Services Council report *School libraries*. While individual schools and schools library services may have clarified their objectives in the intervening ten years, coherent integrated policies embracing the complementary operational roles of these services have in general lagged behind. The schools library service is perhaps the critical link in the pattern of library support for formal education, having in most cases some sort of formal structural relationship with the public library on the one hand, and on the other, an operational relationship with the schools which it serves.

In its role as the only objective source of professional advice available to teachers, the schools library service has the capacity to influence the development of libraries in schools, to ensure that the library is recognised as the centre of information provision in support of the curriculum, and to advise teachers on a range of issues from book selection to in-service training. Another avenue for influence has opened more recently with the accreditation of librarians from several authorities as lay inspectors within the Office for Standards in Education school inspection programme.

Northamptonshire Learning Resources for Education
Flexible Learning Co-ordinator

It should be noted, however, that it is only in large schools library services that the level of staffing can be achieved that can accommodate advisory work to schools on any real scale, and that achievement of this scale is threatened by the splitting up of English counties proposed under local government reform. (See also 4.3.3).

5.6 Development of public library services

As we concluded in Section 3, the potential of the public library as a force in support of reading and information literacy cannot be too strongly emphasised. Its importance lies in ensuring that the reading habit is developed at an early age and is maintained into and beyond the teenage years.

The key role of special areas and targeted service for young people have been recognised in new central libraries, for example, at Croydon. Among older libraries, recognition is manifested in new, improved or enhanced facilities for children that are being created by rebuilding, refurbishment and rethinking.

> **Birmingham Library Services**
> Centre for the Child in the City
>
> **Newcastle upon Tyne City Libraries and Arts**
> Scotswood Library Family Learning Centre

5.6.1 Access to services

Access is not a problem solely of distant static service points, reduced opening hours, and inconvenient mobile library stops. In some library authorities, the make-up of the population requires that, in addition to static and mobile service points, a different approach from these traditional ones is necessary to reach people, including children, in the community, and hence the development of outreach programmes which take the library into the community, making it available in non-library settings, and providing a useful point of contact with many children, parents and carers who would not, for a variety of reasons, visit a public library building.

> **London Borough of Lambeth**
> Outreach Programme
>
> **Somerset County Library**
> Service to Playgroups and Portage Groups

The problem of access to static service points is not one that will go away overnight, or perhaps even at all, but it has led to various alternative methods of delivering service, particularly in rural areas.

> **Norfolk Library and Information Service**
> Village Shops Project
> West Norfolk Projects: Village Green Storytimes
> and Great Western Book Trail
>
> **Nottinghamshire County Libraries**
> Holiday Mobile Service

All public libraries, in rural and urban areas, support their static service points with mobile library services. Because of the fixed schedules to which these operate, their calling times are often during school hours when children are not able to use them. An extension of the standard mobile service is the 'bookbus' service introduced in some authorities which aims specifically to bring books to children in areas that are some distance from branch libraries and, so far as children are concerned, not adequately served by the mobile service.

Cynon Valley Borough Library
Readabout Bookbus

Leicestershire Libraries and Information Service
Bookbus

5.6.2 Promotion of literacy

The importance of the public library in the development of literacy and enjoyment of reading among children from the very earliest age has been described and emphasised in 3.5. We reiterate it here. Children are our future and if libraries cannot get them interested in reading and using libraries the adult readers of tomorrow will be lost and with them the whole notion of a literate, civilised and humane society of which libraries are an integral part.

Birmingham Library Services
Brightstart Early Literacy Project
Beginning with Books Video

Gloucestershire County Library
Grow with Books

5.6.3 Promotion of books and reading

The majority of public libraries nowadays take part in, or run themselves, at least one form of promotional activity during the year, often linked to school summer holidays. Summer book trails are relatively common, for example, at Bexley and Croydon in London; Devon, among others, has been successful in attracting commercial sponsorship. Activities may be linked to a theme as in Humberside with its "Around the world in 80 books" promotion; or to a local author, as in Edinburgh which, in 1994, linked its Treasure Trail to the concurrent Robert Louis Stevenson centenary celebrations in the city, and in North Tyneside which devised the Robert Westall Trail in 1994, with a three-mile trail along the River Tyne featuring many landmarks in Westall's Tyneside books.

Family reading groups, pioneered in Hertfordshire, have now been replicated in numerous other parts of the country, though not with uniform success. Bradford's Book Flood has been tried in Thetford, Norfolk. Humberside's Rhyming Roadshow in 1993 promoted poetry specifically.

We have found, too, many examples of exciting and often entrepreneurial promotional activities in public libraries, some of them mounted in conjunction with private sector companies or with commercial sponsorship. Some of these have become established events in the calendar.

Nottinghamshire Children's Book Award

Northern Children's Book Festival

Greater Manchester Children's Book Festival

Young Gloucestershire Writes

We conclude from these, and many other initiatives which have been drawn to our attention, that **promotion of books and the enjoyment of reading through activities such as those referred to in this and the preceding sections is an integral and vital part of the public library's service to children and young people**.

5.6.4 Support for education, and liaison with schools

Liaison between teachers in schools and librarians in public libraries in matters of practical provision is clearly a matter of concern to many libraries; in the public library, liaison is not necessarily confined to the children's service but may, and often does, extend to reference and local studies collections and to small community libraries without any special collections. There is evidence from individual public libraries that lack of liaison between teachers and public librarians regarding the requirements of the National Curriculum can lead to unreasonable and unacceptable demands being made upon reference and local studies libraries and on local service points.

Pressure on local studies collections in particular has been severe – in Bolton, for example, use of the local studies collection has increased by 30% due to educational demand – and this is especial cause for concern since the fragile nature of much local studies material renders it unsuitable for heavy use. Increased demand for statistical and local studies information leads to increasing use by young people of adult reference libraries which do not always have material at the right level, or the ability to offer the required level of assistance. Many libraries (particularly smaller service points) find the increasing information demands of children very difficult and expensive to serve, and as children usually want information instantly it is often difficult to use back-up resources effectively.

A public library has a fundamental obligation to respond to the demands of any individual young user within its area, for books and for information, and should endeavour to satisfy that demand. Heavy simultaneous pressure on a small number of resources, unrealistic timetables for homework needs, too little warning from schools when demand is about to be generated, mean that many libraries, particularly the smaller service points, are unable to respond satisfactorily.

The failure of the public library in these situations to fulfil the expectations created in children by their teachers has led to the unfortunate perception among these children that the public library does not, or can not, meet their needs. If the public library is unable or unwilling to supply the children's needs, it is likely that they will perceive this as a more general failure to meet their needs, a perception which carries over to other uses and into later life. In addition, curriculum changes impacting on the time available for classes to visit the public library reduces the opportunity for the library service to market its range of services to young and potential users in a cost-effective way.

Many of these problems can be obviated or circumvented through better liaison between teachers and public librarians and pre-planning of supply to meet forecast demand. The ability of teachers to plan the curriculum one year ahead can be a positive factor in pre-planning, as can the willingness of libraries to pre-package material for which there is a known demand. That good and constructive relationships between public libraries and the schools in their areas can and do exist, even in situations of constrained resources on both sides, is manifested by the evidence supplied to the Working Party.

Havering Library Service
Local Studies Information Packs

Bolton Environmental Education Project

Shropshire Libraries
Education Liaison Officer

Staffordshire County Library
PALS: Pre-Admission Libraries in Schools

5.6.5 Under fives

The public library's service to children under five is regarded as one of its major opportunities and challenges. It is the only statutory library service to this age group and the importance of parents and carers who control a young child's access to the library service cannot be over-estimated. There is opportunity for service delivery through the infrastructure of parent and toddler groups and playgroups, and for the public library to provide training for carers of under fives. In view of the limited mobility of under fives, promotion and outreach are the key to service delivery. In these influential years, exposure to the pleasures of reading and stories are critical to develop that drive and hunger necessary in the process of learning to read. Exposure to a range of books including quality writing and illustration at the youngest age is essential. In addition, guidance to parents and carers through targeted collections is widespread already and such information should be integral to service provision to the under fives and their carers.

Knowsley Leisure Services Department
KUFLINC Under Fives Project

Hampshire County Library
Early Years Initiative
Family Library Link

London Borough of Lambeth
Training for Pre-school Playgroups Association Courses

5.6.6 Primary school children

It has been acknowledged that the child's need for guidance in reading comes most particularly between the ages of 7 and 11, or during the primary school years. A number of libraries have targeted this group, frequently in co-operation with the education department, school teachers, school libraries and schools library services, and often involving children, authors and other individuals.

Gloucestershire County Library
Primary School Group Librarians Project

Sunderland Leisure, Libraries and Arts Section
Creative Writing Programmes

5.6.7 Teenagers

Teenage library and information services in authorities such as Renfrew, Bradford (X-change), Glasgow (Yoker) and Gloucestershire (Teenextra) have been established for many years and have been well publicised. The recognition that it is during the teenage years that children are most likely to reduce or stop the reading habit has caused a large number of libraries to review their provision for this age group, in some cases to carry out local surveys of their requirements, and to meet these requirements in new or revamped areas of their libraries, with specially-targeted stock, or in separate developments such as information shops (see 5.6.10).

London Borough of Bromley
'UpFront' Teenage Libraries

Trafford Metropolitan District Libraries
Teenage Library at Coppice Avenue Branch Library

Hertfordshire Libraries, Arts and Information
For Teenagers by Teenagers: Creating a Teenage Library
with the Local Community

Warwickshire County Library Service
'Pages': the Alternative Library

5.6.8 Children with special needs

Children are individuals and while some have clearly identifiable special needs such
as those arising from, for example, hearing or sight impairment, others have more
particular needs that require a range of solutions. It is important for libraries to work
in partnership with other concerned agencies – and with the children themselves –
in order to meet their library and information requirements in the most appropriate
way. As we emphasised in 1.4, children and young people have been taken
throughout this report as including those of minority ethnic origins, those with
disabilities, and others whose needs may be regarded as being in some way special. It
is important that books and other materials reflect back a child's worth and sense of
value, and that they are enabled to make use of the library and its services in whatever
way is appropriate.

Cumbria County Library
Disadvantaged Children using a Public Library Service
(Public Library Development Incentive Scheme (PLDIS) funded project)

Gloucestershire County Library
Special Needs Initiative 1993/95

Hampshire County Library
Southampton Bookbus

Gwent Libraries
Mobile Toy Library for Children with Special Needs

5.6.9 Information technology

A comprehensive survey of the provision of audiovisual and computer (AVC) materials for young people by public libraries and schools library services in 1989 suggested that "public libraries in Britain have done little to equip young people for a life in which the computer is a major element in learning, work and recreation".[11] It was found that while provision of audiovisual material was relatively high in both types of service, provision of computer software to support the varying degrees of hardware availability was uniformly low, and access to it was diminished by factors such as availability at a very small number of service points, the holding of collections on closed access, minimum age restrictions on use, and insistence on in-house use. The main reasons for poor provision were found to be lack of funding, and a widespread view that responsibility for provision of computer materials lay elsewhere.

While some improvement in overall provision was found two years after the main survey, continuing funding problems in young people's services and the effects of Local Management of Schools on schools library services make future plans less than firm. We draw attention again to the authors' conclusions. "The full spectrum of recreational needs of young people in the electronic age is not being addressed by libraries. This failing is unlikely to encourage the customers of tomorrow to use the services of today. It is slowly marginalising libraries into providers of print-based resources."[12]

Although books have a chronological importance in a child's life and must remain as an important element in library services for children and young people, we believe that **public libraries should not be seen as totally book-orientated**. Children nowadays are accustomed to using computers and multimedia formats for both recreation and information; their high use of OPACs (online public access catalogues) in public libraries has also been noted, and their perception of the public library as a place that is 'switched on' to technology needs to be exploited.

Gloucestershire County Library
MERLIN (formerly THEMIS): 'Kids' Corner'

Book Wizard
A new multimedia children's book selection programme

Southwark Library Services
CD-Roms in all Libraries

Wolverhampton Libraries
IT Developments for Children

5.6.10 Partnerships

Lack of formal channels of communication between local authority departments on library matters is all too often a reality, and it can be argued that strategic development, liaison and mutual support between the public library and other parts of the council have been made more difficult with the creation of business units and the client/contractor split. It is probably true to say that examples of developments involving the library and one or more other council departments are principally small-scale and practical. But of these practical developments, there are numerous examples, some of which are referred to in other sections of this report, for example, Northamptonshire's Learning Resources for Education (5.5) Lambeth's outreach programme (5.6.1) and Gwent's mobile toy library (5.6.8).

Nottinghamshire County Library
Youth Information Shop, Mansfield Library

Recent legislation such as the Children Act and programmes such as Care in the Community can give an impetus to co-operation and, in the case of the Children Act, positively require council departments to co-operate on strategies for meeting their needs through services across the board. National initiatives such as the Child Friendly City also provide a framework within which inter-departmental programmes and projects can be made to work.

Council-wide responsibilities in providing services for children can be formalised through a multi-service Charter setting out the boundaries of reasonable expectation on the part of a child for service in general delivered through the local authority and its components and agencies. Such a charter would include the child's right to access to books paid for from the education budget as part of his/her education together with the right of access through the public library service to books and information in support of his/her development as a literate human being. The process of developing such a charter can in itself stimulate initiatives appropriate to local circumstances which can be commended to all local bodies, including schools, that are accountable to the local community through their services, and assist them in attaining standards to meet expectations.

London Borough of Sutton
Up to Standard: Corporate Statement including:
Standards for Services for the Under Fives
Standards for Services for Children and Young People

Bedfordshire County Council
Under Eights Service:
'Children First' Early Childhood Charter

5.6.11 Inter-agency development

Partnerships with statutory and voluntary sector organisations such as Kids Club Network, Early Years Liaison Groups, local branches of Action with Communities in Rural England (ACRE) (formerly the Rural Development Council) and health and education provider organisations are noted in numerous authorities of all types. The voluntary sector may come to play a more important part in assessing needs and acting as a partner; childminders and carers will be more significant and require services from the public library in connection with encouraging young children in their care to read and enjoy books. Increasing professionalisation of local voluntary sector activity can provide opportunities for further dialogue and the potential for joint working.

Opportunities to research and develop services through an inter-agency approach should be considered and explored.

Bookstart
Pilot Project in Birmingham

Northamptonshire Libraries and Information Service
Kids' Club Network
Development with Early Years Liaison Groups

North Tyneside Libraries
ALBSU Family Literacy Demonstration Programme:
Parents and Children Together (PACT)

Key conclusions

- The public library service in general is not adequately resourced to make up for the deficiencies of educational institutions that can not or will not provide sufficient textbooks and library books for their own pupils, nor does it have professional specialist staff in sufficient numbers to cope with the additional demands from pupils who are often inadequately briefed by teachers and unable to use books and other information sources for themselves. [5.2]

- An integrated strategy for delivery of library services for children and young people through individual school libraries, the schools library service, and the public library, is necessary to support the needs of the National Curriculum, and broader educational needs both in and out of school. The integrated strategy should be devised and owned by the local authority and its components and agencies to meet the needs of its local community of children. [5.2]

- We are convinced of the need for co-ordination at national level, which will also encourage integrated strategies at local level. [5.2]

- The role of the public library in meeting the needs of children and young people is of paramount importance to the future economic and cultural health of this country. Continuation of its service to them, untrammelled by barriers to access such as charging, is a critical factor in the future development of the public library service as a whole. [5.3]

- What children should be entitled to from a core public library service should be spelled out in a charter specifically relating to children. [5.3.1]

- At a time of continuing pressure on resources, a library has to identify its priorities within the overall needs of children and young people, and to endeavour to meet them through its aims and objectives. Objectives for children's services should reflect the integral part that promotion and outreach play in service delivery. [5.3.2]

- We cannot see the imposition of national standards as a realistic goal. But the Library Association's current project to develop model standards for public libraries is endorsed as producing helpful professional guidance which can be adapted for use locally. We hope that the standards may contain some explicit statements regarding the importance of services for children and young people as a core element in the public library's function. [5.3.3]

- Centrally conceived manuals of performance indicators are unlikely to gain general acceptability. But there should be some guidance on performance indicators at national level which can be adapted for use locally as required. [5.3.4]

- A proper survey methodology, capable of being applied nationally, is critical to any understanding of the extent to which public libraries are meeting the needs of children and young people. [5.3.4]

- The majority of the recommendations of the Library and Information Services Council report on school libraries remain valid in broad terms. [5.4]

- There should be a requirement upon schools to demonstrate how they will provide adequate learning resources to underpin the teaching of the National Curriculum. But a consensus on what constitutes adequacy in school library provision will not emerge unless the criteria contained in the Office for Standards in Education *Handbook* for use in inspections are expanded, sharpened, and made more explicit. [5.4]

- The school library is an integral part of curriculum planning for reading and information handling throughout the whole school. [5.4] Particularly in the secondary school, it is the natural base for the teaching of information skills. [5.4.1]

- The future of schools library services must be safeguarded: the impact on school libraries, and on the public library service, should existing services be run down would be immensely damaging. [5.5]

- Promotion of books and the enjoyment of reading is an integral and vital part of the public library's service to children and young people. [5.6.1, 5.6.2, 5.6.3]

- Public libraries should not be seen as totally book-orientated but should offer relevant multimedia materials to meet the reasonable expectations of young people. [5.6.9]

- Council-wide responsibilities in providing services for children can be formalised through a multi-service charter setting out the boundaries of reasonable expectation on the part of a child for service. [5.6.10]

- Opportunities to research and develop services through an inter-agency approach should be considered and explored. [5.6.11]

Recommendations

■ Each local authority should publish an integrated strategy for delivering library and information services to meet the identified needs of children and young people throughout its area, taking into account the roles, relationships and responsibilities of the major elements in the service – the public library, the schools library service, and libraries in individual schools – and involving other agencies as appropriate, eg, further education colleges, Training and Enterprise Councils. [5.2]

   The strategy should take due account of recognised standards relating to services for children and young people. [5.3.3]

   Inspection and monitoring should form a part of the strategy. [5.2]

   – Chief Executives of Local Authorities with education and library functions; DNH; DFE; OFSTED; TECs

■ The new Library and Information Commission should advise Government regarding its national role in support of libraries and information services for children and young people. [5.2]

   – DNH (Library and Information Commission)

■ The satisfaction of children's and young people's needs as individuals should be recognised and promoted as a core element of the public library service, central to its role in the promotion of literacy and its role in relation to educational institutions as defined in Recommendation 1. [5.3]

   – DNH (Review of the Public Library Service); Library Managers

■ There must be clear objectives for services to children and young people, and clear priorities should be established for children's needs across ages and stages of development. The objectives should accommodate the promotion of services to the child population as an integral and vital part of service provision, and should acknowledge the duty of public libraries to work with parents and carers of young children. [2, 5.3.2, 5.6.3]

   – Library Managers

■ The DNH should initiate work on a model charter which can be adapted for local use and published by public libraries as a Charter for the Reader relating to children and their needs. Such a charter might include the responsibilities of the organisation to ensure that staff are adequately trained, to provide accessible service and customer care in relation to children, and to properly investigate the needs of children and their parents and carers, recognising the differing needs of different age groups, backgrounds and stages of development. [5.3.1]

   – DNH; Library Managers; LA

■ There should be model standards for services for children and young people, specifying minimum levels of provision and entitlement. In order to facilitate their acceptance by local authorities, they should be drawn up by the Library Association in consultation with the local authority associations and the Department of National Heritage. They should be accepted and adapted by local authorities as part of their statutory responsibility to provide services for children through public libraries. Their application should be monitored by DNH as part of its overall monitoring responsibilities. [5.3.3]

– LA; Library Managers; DNH; LISU

■ The Department of National Heritage should take the lead in the development of national performance indicators which reflect the rights and entitlements of children, and include at least a basic indicator for a child's rights to reading materials and library services. [5.3.4]

A model set of performance indicators specific to children's services, which will measure performance against defined objectives, taking into account quality aspects that are important to the user, should be developed for local use where indicators are not already in place in the local authority. [5.3.4]

– DNH; Audit Commission

■ The public library has a duty to meet children's need and desire for information in a range of media as well as books. It should provide information in appropriate media and formats, and whatever technology is needed to deliver them, and should promote their availability and use. [5.6.9]

– Library Managers

■ A multi-service Charter for the Child, drawn up jointly by all departments of the local authority that provide services for children, and published by the local authority, should set out the child's entitlement to service in general, including what he or she can reasonably expect from library services as defined in the integrated strategy proposed in Recommendation 1. The charter should be reviewed regularly for the relevance and currency of its content, and its impact should be monitored. [5.6.10]

– Local Authorities; School Governing Bodies

References

1. ASLIB CONSULTANCY. *DNH review of the public library service in England and Wales: preliminary information, August 1994.* Aslib, 1994.
2. MYERS, John. Stable, quiet retreats, or bustling with innovation? *Library Association Record* 96(8) August 1994, 426-427.
3. LIBRARY ASSOCIATION. *Children and young people: Library Association guidelines for public library services.* Library Association Publishing Ltd, 1991.
4. SUMSION, John. *Practical performance indicators – 1992: documenting the Citizens' Charter consultation for UK public libraries with examples of PIs and surveys in use.* Loughborough, LISU, 1993.
5. LIBRARY AND INFORMATION SERVICES COUNCIL (ENGLAND). *School libraries: the foundations of the curriculum.* HMSO, 1984. Library information series no.13.
6. OFFICE FOR STANDARDS IN EDUCATION. *Handbook for the inspection of schools;* May 1994 amendment. HMSO, 1994.

7. CHILDREN'S LITERATURE RESEARCH CENTRE. *Contemporary juvenile reading habits: a study of young people's reading at the end of the century.* Roehampton Institute, CLRC, 1994.

8. SCOTTISH OFFICE EDUCATION DEPARTMENT. *Information and study skills in Scottish secondary schools: a report by HM Inspectors of Schools.* Edinburgh, HMSO, 1991.

9. SCOTTISH OFFICE EDUCATION DEPARTMENT *op. cit.*

10. HEEKS, Peggy and KINNELL, Margaret. *Managing change for school library services: the final report of the Supports to Learning Project.* British Library, 1992. Library and Information Research report 89.

11. LONSDALE, Ray and WHEATLEY, Alan. The provision of computer material and services to young people by British public libraries. *Journal of Librarianship and Information Science,* 24 (2) June 1992, 87-98.

12. LONSDALE and WHEATLEY *op. cit.*

Appendix A
Members of the Working Party

Chairman	David Leabeater	National Consumer Council
Members	Tudfil Adams	LISC (Wales)
	Peter Beauchamp	Department of National Heritage
	Wendy Cooling	Children's Book Consultant
	Gillian Cross	Children's Author
	Yvonne Gill-Martin	Assistant Chief Librarian, Bolton Metropolitan District
	Vivien Griffiths	Acting Senior Assistant Director, Birmingham Library Services
	Grace Kempster	Assistant Head of Libraries and Arts, London Borough of Richmond upon Thames
	Chris Kloet	Editorial Director, Children's Books, Victor Gollancz
	David Lathrope	Assistant Director, Leisure Services (Libraries), Nottinghamshire County Library Service
	Michael Marland	Head Teacher, North Westminster Community School
	Martin Molloy	Principal Librarian, Service Development, Derbyshire Library Services
	Margaret Morrissey	Public Relations Officer, National Confederation of Parent Teacher Associations
	Mary Nettlefold	TC Farries and Co
	Margaret Smith	Head of Service, Cambridgeshire Schools Library Service
	Hadrian Southorn	Vice Chairman, National Association of School Governors and Managers
	Doug Taylor	General Manager, National Union of Students of the UK
	Verna Taylor	County Librarian, Northamptonshire Libraries and Information Service
Secretary	Brenda White	Principal Consultant, Brenda White Associates
Assessors	Lesley Blundell	Department of National Heritage
	John Burchell	British Library Research and Development Department
	Stewart Robertson	Office for Standards in Education
	John Tucker	Department for Education
Observer	Vincent O'Hara	LISC (Northern Ireland)

Appendix B
Organisations invited to submit evidence or information

Association of London Chief Librarians

Association of Metropolitan District Chief Librarians

Association of Metropolitan District Education and Children's Librarians

Booksellers' Association: Children's Book Group, School Suppliers Group

British Association for Early Childhood Education

British Association of Information and Library Education and Research

Children's Literature Research Centre, Roehampton Institute

Colleges of Further and Higher Education (group of the Library Association)

Education Librarians' Group (of the Library Association)

Educational Publishers' Council

Federation of Children's Book Groups

Federation of Local Authority Chief Librarians

Library and Information Statistics Unit, Loughborough University of Technology

National Children's Bureau

Pre-school Playgroups Association

Publishers' Association: Children's Book Group

School Library Association

School Libraries Group (of the Library Association)

Society of County Children's and Education Librarians

Society of County Librarians

Youth and Education Librarians London

Youth Libraries Group (of the Library Association)

Appendix C
Examples of service initiatives

Note: All details, contact names and telephone numbers are correct as at September 1994. The numbering and order of sections follows that of the main report.

2.2 Library needs of children and young people

Waltham Forest Libraries and Arts Department

Teenagers and libraries: a study in Waltham Forest

One of the best-known local surveys, which was well conducted, reported and publicised, was the survey of 990 Waltham Forest library users aged between 11 and 23, carried out in 1985. It showed a high level of use of libraries by teenagers in the sample, use remaining high while teenagers are in education but dropping rapidly as soon as they leave school or college. The findings represent a profile of need and demand to which library resources for teenage groups could be adjusted, for example, a different approach and image may be necessary for older teenage boys, the content of teenage sections need to be improved.

Published report: Title as above

Contact: Jerry Hurst, Head of Young People's Library Services, (0181) 556 8600

Southwark Library Services

Survey of Primary School Children in the Borough

The most recent survey, ambitious and carefully-planned, was that carried out by Southwark Library Services who sent a questionnaire during National Library Week 1993 to children in primary schools (aged 5 to 11) in the borough asking questions (piloted in a sample of schools to get the questions right) about reading and use of public libraries. The questionnaire was returned by some 2,000 children, thus getting non-library users into the net as well as users. Responses were analysed using a database package developed in conjunction with the Council's IT section, to give information library by library across the borough, and by age and gender.

Information coming out of the survey demonstrates how popular the local library is, what children use it for, what they think of it, what its most popular features are, and what children want from their library. In the main the analysis confirms rather than illuminates, although there are some surprises. The findings will influence service delivery and inform stock selection in the borough. A published report is planned.

Contact: Sue Moody, Youth and Education Librarian, (0171) 525 2830

4.1.6 Education and training of staff

Gwent Libraries

In-service and Co-operative Training

The 'Children are Customers' course is attended by all Gwent Libraries staff.

It introduces staff to the county's services to children, youth services and schools library services, services for children with special needs, promotional activities and events. The course folder incorporates youth services aims and objectives, standards for services to young people including performance measurements, and customer care points taken from the Library Association guidelines.

A co-operative venture, SET, involving South Glamorgan Library, Newport Borough Libraries and Gwent Libraries organises training courses for staff of the three library authorities, and further afield. Gwent was responsible for organising a two-day course on marketing library services to children under the title 'Kids Count', working from an author/reviewer point of view through to publishing and bookselling, and then looking in detail at library marketing with examples of good practice and including co-operation between suppliers and libraries. Seven library suppliers supported the course by helping with promotion and funding of speakers, delegate packs, badges, and displays at the accompanying exhibition.

Contact: Ann Jones, Principal Librarian: Youth Services, (01633) 832437

Yorkshire Children's Services Group

An informal gathering of heads of children's and education services from the metropolitan districts of South and West Yorkshire which meets approximately every six weeks to exchange ideas and information and initiate joint ventures which benefit from co-operative resourcing. Such ventures include good quality publicity, for example on the importance of schools library services aimed at school governors; and promotional activities, for example a summer holiday reading game in 1994 for which 600,000 leaflets were distributed to every child of primary school age throughout Yorkshire. At least one training event is held every year on topics of a practical nature. In summer 1994, training on children with special needs was given on two successive days, the first aimed at librarians and the second at teachers.

Contact: Steve Hird, Principal Librarian, Youth and Schools Services, Rotherham Libraries, Museum and Arts Department, (01709) 813034

Greater Manchester Public Library Training Co-operative
Co-operative Training

A co-operative venture, set up in the late 1980s to address the need for training within the constituent authorities, using in the main local expertise that exists within the group. It arranges courses on topics such as "Customers with special needs: Children".

The aims of the group are:
1. to heighten awareness of library training and development in Greater Manchester library authorities;
2. to improve services to the public by providing better trained staff;
3. to enable a co-ordinated and systematic approach to library training;
4. to maximise use of local resources and share costs of facilities for training;
5. to meet needs of authorities where possible by the provision of training courses or acting as a clearing house for training in the area or region.

Contact: Barbara Harlock, Secretary, (0161) 911 4644

4.2.4 Education and training by University LIS Schools

Leeds Metropolitan University

Professional Diploma in School Library Studies

The current Professional Diploma offered by the Information and Library Studies Group has evolved from the former Certificate in School Library Studies, and is a three-module course within the university's short course programme. Initially designed to be offered for use on-site, lack of take-up necessitated a change of route and it is currently being used by Tameside MBC Inspection and Advisory Service as a semi-distance learning package for teachers running school libraries. It is on offer to other authorities if required and can be bought as a standard package, or negotiated to suit individual requirements. A survey is planned, using the journal *School Librarian*, to ascertain if there is a market for a proper distance learning package; if there is, funding and resources will have to be found for it.

Tameside have run it as a three module course with certification, and students are currently completing module 3. The first module, with a very practical assessment of preparing a policy for a school library, attracted 20 teachers; for the second module, with a broader focus of the library in the school and as part of the curriculum, the number dropped to ten; three are now taking the third module leading to the Diploma. Experience is that it has been a very useful course. The first and second modules had some support from both the Inspection and Advisory Service and the schools library service, and the course has provided the impetus for setting up a network of school librarians facilitated by the schools library service.

Contact: Sally Gibbs, Senior Lecturer, Information and Library Studies Group, Leeds Metropolitan University, (0113) 283 2600 ext. 3552

Chris Threlfall, General Adviser, English, Tameside Inspection and Advisory Service, (0161) 342 3246

University of Central England

In-service Training Courses

The School of Information Studies can provide courses in aspects of school and children's librarianship and literature which can be specially packaged to meet the requirements of individual libraries and held on their premises. In-house courses have been run for, among others, Bromley, Hammersmith and Fulham, and Wandsworth, and subjects covered have included CD-Roms in schools, user education and information skills, children's fiction, and teenage services.

In the main, courses have been organised as a result of personal contacts, but the School of Information Studies would welcome enquiries from public or school libraries regarding their staff training needs.

Contact: Judith Elkin, Head, School of Information Studies, University of Central England, (0121) 331 5625

5.2 Strategy for service delivery

North Tyneside Libraries

Children and Young People's Library Service

An integrated strategy for delivering a quality library service to children and young people is firmly at the heart of North Tyneside policy. A council restructuring in 1992 gave the opportunity to integrate the former schools library service with the public library service and establish the new Children and Young People's (CYP) team. This team co-ordinates the delivery of the library service to children and young people, taking their needs as the central and paramount factor. The main premise is that the same potential client group of children go to school and may use the public libraries in any given community and that their library needs in both places are not wildly different. The CYP team works on a 'patch' basis, each CYP librarian overseeing the public library service points, the pre-school, school and community needs of the CYP customer group in their 'patch'. The principle is now firmly in place, and consolidation will take place over the coming years; CYP policy guidelines, currently in draft form, outline in greater detail the philosophy outlined above.

Contact: Jan Clements, Manager of CYP Library Service, (0191) 268 9999

Cambridgeshire County Council

Public Library Services to Schools: Service Level Agreement with Cambridgeshire Schools Library Service

A. Public libraries **will** provide:

Core services

1. Loan of books and other material to children and teachers as individual library users.
2. Provision of information and reference material to children and teachers as individual library users.
3. Advice about books and reading development as to any adult carer.
4. Display facilities for work by pupils where possible.
5. Loan collection of materials to under fives groups.

Specialist Advice Services

1. User education through group visits to libraries.
2. Promotional visits by library staff to schools.

B. Public libraries will **not** provide:

1. Special loan facilities or requests for teachers.
2. Bulk loans to teachers.
3. Advice to schools on setting up or maintaining a library.
4. Stock editing and classification in schools.

Contact: Margaret Smith, Head of Service, Cambridgeshire Schools Library Service, (01480) 436465

Northumberland Schools Library Service

Service Level Agreements

Northumberland Schools Library Service's funding was delegated in 1993, and its remaining central funding was removed by budget reductions in 1994. It therefore has no delegated money at all, and must earn all of its income. It operates three types of service level agreements: the standard one with local education authority (LEA) schools in the county; an agreement with non-school users of services such as the Advisory and Inspection Division and reading centres; and an agreement with (so far) one school in a neighbouring LEA area.

The Service Agreement for Educational Resource Material, into which LEA schools in Northumberland are invited to enter, emphasises that "the scheme only aims to supplement the individual provision made by schools". It specifies six levels of available service in terms of resource entitlement (items per pupil) and staff time, and the charges for these for first, middle, high and special schools; service levels above those specified can be provided on a pro rata basis, and a minimum charge applies.

Contact: Martin Stone, Principal Libraries Officer (Education and Agency Services), (01670) 511156

US National Commission on Libraries and Information Science

The US National Commission on Libraries and Information Science is a permanent federal agency which advises Congress and President on library and information matters. Its current initiatives regarding the federal role in support of library and information services and literacy programmes for children and young people arise from the Omnibus Children and Youth Literacy Initiative (a priority recommendation from the 1991 White House Conference on Library and Information Services) and its main areas of concern, as identified, lie very close to those identified by this Working Party:

- the critical role of library and information services in supporting attainment of national education goals;
- the relationship between library and information services and related education and training programmes;
- the need for statistics on the status of library and information services for children and young people and for research into the relationship between student performance and the quality of school library media centre services;
- the need for public awareness of the contribution and the needs of library and information services for children and young people.

Contact: Peter R Young, Director, US National Commission on Libraries and Information Science, 1110 Vermont Avenue NW, Suite 820, Washington, DC 20005-3522, (00 1 202) 606 9200

5.3.1 Charter for children

South Eastern Education and Library Board, Northern Ireland
'Our Promise to Children'

As part of its Policy Review of Library Services to Children and Young People, June 1993, the South Eastern Education and Library Board of Northern Ireland set out "Our Promise to Children" as follows:

We promise ...
- to listen
  to what you have to say about your library;

- to explain
  how the library works and how to use it;
- to help
  you find the books and information you need;
- to provide
  the best books for you to enjoy;
- to encourage
  you to read as widely and as often as possible.

We will do our best to make your library a ...
- safe
- attractive
- friendly
  ... place for you and your family to visit.

The Promise is also incorporated into a leaflet *Your child and the Library* which sets out the responsibilities of the Library:

- to ensure that the library is a safe, attractive and welcoming place for you and your child;
- to be fair but firm in dealing with children who disturb or upset other library users;
- to take reasonable care of all children on our premises. Your pre-school child must be accompanied by an adult or a responsible older brother or sister;
- to ensure that all our children's activities are well organised and properly supervised;
- to help your child to understand and use the library and obtain the resources or information she/he needs;
- to provide a varied and balanced stock carefully selected by well trained staff.

Contact: Laura Plummer, Assistant Chief Librarian, Education and Young People's Services, (01238) 562639

London Borough of Bromley
'The Child as Customer'
Bromley has a customer charter for adults, and management has agreed that a similar charter should be drawn up specifically for children. This is in preparation.
Contact: Pat Jones, Youth Services Manager, (0181) 460 9955

5.3.2 Aims and objectives

Nottinghamshire County Library Service
Public Library Services to Children: Aims, Objectives and Performance Indicators

Children are defined here as all young people from babies up to and including 13-year-olds.

There is a single over-arching service aim, followed by seven objectives. Performance indicators comprise eight customer-based, six stock-based, one expenditure-based, and three others covering information enquiries and children's activities.

Contact: Philip Marshall, Principal Libraries Officer: Client Services, (0115) 985 4201

5.3.3 **Standards**

Berkshire Department of Libraries, Archives and Tourism

Specification for Children's Services in Public Libraries

The specification covers customers, core service, stock, staffing, accommodation, and promotion, with performance indicators for each.

Contact: Andrew Stevens, Quality Manager, (01734) 233282

Birmingham Library Services (Community Services)

Service Level Agreement with the Children, Youth and Education Team

The Children, Youth and Education Team (CYE) exists to provide support to the rest of Birmingham Library Services in the delivery of a quality service to children and young people, their parents and carers and to teachers and schools. The potential scale of demand required that a definitive statement be made in the form of a Service Level Agreement (SLA) of the scope and level of service that clients can expect. The SLA defines the framework within which the team operates and its expectations of the clients' responses.

The areas of service covered by the Agreement are:
– communication;
– training and professional support;
– book selection and approval service;
– promotion and image;
– role of the Central Children's Library;
– role of the schools library service.

The Agreement is monitored on a quarterly basis by a customer panel, a joint working group of CYE Team and Community Service staff, and minor adjustments can be made as necessary. There are 15 performance measures. Following a major restructuring of the Library Services, work on reviewing the Agreement is now under way.

Contact: Patsy Heap, Principal Officer, Children Youth and Education Services, (0121) 235 2418.

5.3.4 **Quality assessment and performance measurement**

Kent Arts and Libraries

Quality Standards

"Written standards are the most visible and concrete expression of quality assurance in Arts and Libraries. They formalise best practice and bring consistency to a large, devolved organisation, without imposing an unnecessary degree of uniformity. They also:
– let customers know what to expect of us;
– let staff know what is expected of them;
– allow training to be structured around them."

Kent's Quality Management Group takes each standard through a six-stage process of commissioning, drafting, commenting, revising, piloting and consultation, and authorising, ie, issuing the standard for implementation in the Department.

Quality Standards cover stock provision for young people; promoting reading and library skills to young people. The complete set is available from Kent Arts and Libraries at a cost of £10.

Contact: Stephen Sage, Head of Client Services, (01622) 605210

Norfolk Library and Information Service
Quality Statements

Norfolk's Standards of Customer Service state that "The library and information service provides access to knowledge to enable Norfolk people to enjoy learning, leisure and thinking in a safe and welcoming environment. It invests in staff who are committed to providing a high quality service which meets individuals' reading and information needs, at good value for money." In respect of children, it states that "We will encourage children to read by arranging reading games and similar activities and by providing quality children's books in pleasant surroundings."

Norfolk also has produced separate quality statements on the public library's service to children and young people, and on the schools library service, together with a protocol agreement between the schools library service and the public young people's service.

Contact: Dorne Fraser, Senior Librarian, Young People's Services, (01603) 222270

Westminster Libraries
Quality Inspection Schedule

Westminster Libraries Business Unit 'Westminster Libraries' was created in June 1992 and encompasses all 12 community libraries together with the mobile library and technical services. The Quality Inspection Schedule, revised in January 1994, sets out the required coverage of quality inspections in Westminster Libraries and acts as a guide for the conduct of the inspections. The schedule does not contain precise criteria but sets out headings under which each area being considered (physical environment, etc) will be assessed according to known best practice. Definition of 'adequate' or 'appropriate' standards are regarded as varying from one library to another according to its market and the "legitimate choice of the library manager". Schedule 13 refers to services to children and young people and contains 20 headings for the service in general, seven for class visits by schools, 12 for services to specific groups.

Following a pilot, the inspection process has been applied to St. John's Wood Library in July 1993, Paddington Library in November 1993, and Westminster City Archives (which includes the local history collection) in March/April 1994.

Contact: Iain Watt, Library Contracts Manager, (0171) 798 1838

5.4.1 Information skills

St Aidan's High School, Wishaw, Scotland
Information Skills Programme

An example of an effective information skills programme which has been developed from a TVEI Pilot Initiative on Information Skills run jointly with the Education Resource Service, and in liaison with the Learning Support Department to increase the effective use of resources. The school wanted to make a commitment to the teaching of information skills which would help pupils to approach all types of investigative tasks more effectively. Individual departments took responsibility for teaching a range of information skills, with the Science Department leading the way. Skills targeted initially were chosen for their cross-curricular importance, eg, brainstorming, identifying keywords, using spider diagrams, note-taking, skimming to locate information, organising and presenting information.

A focus was provided by formation of an Information Skills Group consisting of a member of the Senior Management Team, the Resource Librarian, the Principal Teacher of Learning Support, and other members of staff with expertise and enthusiasm. The group was responsible for planning a whole school approach to the teaching of information skills.

Contact: Kathleen Gibbons, Deputy Head Teacher, St. Aidan's High School, (01698) 381888

Clwyd Library and Information Service
School Library and Information Skill Development Project

Clwyd Library and Information Service carried out a school library development project with funding from the Welsh Office Education Department between September 1990 and July 1992. The aim of the project was to develop a strategy for library use within a high school and its family of primary schools and in particular to develop information skills for the purposes of independent study by trialling a model of school library staffing where high schools are linked to their primary feeder schools. Two families of schools were involved in the project. Funding allowed a librarian and library assistant for each family of schools. The project is regarded as having been successful, perhaps less so in terms of the development of information skills than in the appointment of library staff to all high schools in the county. This has raised the profile of the libraries in these schools and has had a positive effect in assuring their continuation; use of the libraries themselves has increased, as has the use by the schools of the county's schools library service.

Contact: David Barker, Principal Librarian, Services to Education and Young People, (01352) 702488

North Tyneside Libraries
INSET for Teachers

North Tyneside has worked for and with its schools for many years, attempting to lead school libraries towards high standards of resource provision and supporting their efforts through a range of in-service training (INSET) and advice. The results of a two-year pilot project (1989/91) aimed at developing information skills were published as *Learning to learn: information skills in the primary school*, which is recommended reading by the Office for Standards in Education. Other in-house publications include *The library file*, a ring binder of guidelines and organisational information for school libraries, and a leaflet *Class visits: learning information skills in your library* which highlights the role to be played by the school library as well as the public library system. The Children and Young People's (CYP) team is also providing expert guidance and support for 12 primary schools which received grants to develop their library through the SLA/Paul Hamlyn Foundation pilot scheme in September 1994.

Contact: Jan Clements, Manager of CYP Library Service, (0191) 268 9999

Bolton Libraries, Arts and Archives
Local Studies Training Day

Bolton Libraries training initiative aimed at schools in the light of demand generated by the National Curriculum. Take-up was mainly from primary schools. During one Monday in January 1994, some 60 teachers visited Local Studies for awareness training on what was available to support classroom teaching.

Contact: Kevin Campbell, Archivist, (01204) 22311

5.5 The role of the schools library service

Northamptonshire Learning Resources for Education
Flexible Learning Co-ordinator

A Flexible Learning Co-ordinator was appointed to Northamptonshire Learning Resources for Education for the period May 1993 to April 1994, to raise awareness of links between resource provision and flexible and independent learning approaches to the curriculum. Working with secondary schools, librarians, and Education Advisory staff, the postholder, who was a trained teacher, provided consultancy and training services to support the information skills aspect of the National Curriculum and the introduction of flexible learning approaches. A particular emphasis was on in-service training and the development and promotion of school learning resource centres and flexible learning packages.

Contact: Kay Harrison, Learning Resources Manager, (01604) 20262

5.6 Development of public library services

Birmingham Library Services
Centre for the Child in the City

Birmingham's Central Children's Library was destroyed by fire in April 1991. The need to rebuild offered a chance for a major reassessment of its role in terms of the needs of children and young people into the year 2000. This reassessment encompassed consultation with a wide range of children, young people, parents and other adults involved in working with and/or caring for children. It resulted in the creation of the Centre for the Child, a unique new concept in library services to children and young people, which opened in autumn 1994.

Key aims of the Centre for the Child include:
- to be a place in the city centre which highlights the importance of the child, which welcomes the child, which is for the child and which encourages an awareness of citizenship in children;
- to celebrate books and reading for pleasure and help parents;
- to provide a gateway to a range of other services for children in the city and their parents and carers;
- to facilitate corporate and co-operative service provision for children and their families.

As well as a main Children's Lending Library, its facilities include a disability resource area, independent learning areas, parent and baby room, two meeting and activity rooms and a childcare information bureau.

Contact: Anne Everall, Principal Librarian, Children's and Youth Services, (0121) 235 2465

Newcastle upon Tyne City Libraries and Arts
Scotswood Library Family Learning Centre

The branch library in Scotswood serves an inner city area of Newcastle which is characterised by high deprivation and unemployment and in which there is a high percentage of single parent families and young children. There is nevertheless a strong community spirit and a desire to work for improvement which has seen one outcome in the refurbishment of Scotswood Library with the help of Urban Programme funding and its transformation into a Family Learning Centre. In this building are housed the library itself, which has been refurbished with features such as face-out shelving and multimedia resources, a pre-school playgroup, and the City Challenge funded 'On with Learning' project to support adults in improving and developing their skills.

Contact: Allan Wraight, Principal Librarian, Community Service, (0191) 261 0691

5.6.1. Access to services

London Borough of Lambeth
Outreach Programme

In addition to 13 libraries throughout the borough and two mobile libraries, all of which offer resources to children and young people, Lambeth Public Library and Archives Services' outreach service provides materials and advice to over 250 community groups in the borough concerned with children and young people. It provides a useful point of contact with many who would not, for a variety of reasons, use library buildings. Visible collections of resources in community buildings and regular visits by library staff result in a high local profile for library services. Feedback from users provides the basis for continuous reassessment of stock and services.

Collections, advice and general support are regularly supplied to groups such as playgroups, day nurseries, one o'clock clubs, parent and toddler groups, after-school and holiday projects, youth clubs and centres, and children's homes, plus a wide range of groups which cater for adults with responsibilities for children, such as women's refuges. Some 40 groups catering for under fives participate in storytelling sessions with storytellers employed by the Library Service. Children with disabilities are served through groups such as community health clinics and specialist playgroups and playgrounds; childminders have access to resources through the Social Services Childminders' Toy Library which receives regular materials and advice from the Library Service. Many other specially tailored services are supplied. Wherever appropriate, children are encouraged to join their local libraries as well as to make use of these community collections.

Contact: Steph Smith, Young People's Services Librarian, (0171) 926 9327

Somerset County Library
Service to Playgroups and Portage Groups

Portage is a step-by-step teaching approach for children with special needs used as part of a home-teaching service. The name comes from Portage in Wisconsin, USA, where the approach was developed in the 60s to provide teaching for children living in rural communities who were delayed in their development; it began to be used in Britain in 1976 as a method of helping under-fives with special needs.

In Somerset, a one-off allocation of money was made in 1991 to the Library Service to redress the shortfall between playgroups actually served in the county and the potential users of the facility to borrow collections of books. All playgroups in the county were contacted by letter and, at the request of the County's Early Years Co-ordinator, the offer was extended to the county's five Portage groups, one teacher from each group being asked to hold the library card for that group, with access to collections of books in the same way as a playgroup. From 129 playgroups in 1988, the number borrowing collections has risen to 257 in 1993/94. Only limited use by Portage groups is reported, but the allowance that they do have is appreciated; although suggestions have been made for special stock items, experience shows that most borrowing is of mainstream stock.

Contact: Rachel Boyd, Manager, Library Services to Education and Young People, (01278) 421015

Norfolk Library and Information Service
Village Shops Project

Norfolk's particular problems of rural dispersion, and the related problem of mobile libraries visiting sites when children are in school, have been tackled through a project in three villages in which the mobile library service was replaced by libraries in village shops. In two of the villages, the shop in which the library is based is the only one in the community; in these two villages, the percentage of children's books borrowed is considerably higher than the average for the rest of the county. In the third village, where there is a fairly wide range of shops, the library is located in the general stores, and in this village the percentage of children's borrowing is slightly less than the county average, and slightly less than half of that in the other two villages. Even so, the shop library in this village has added 109% to children's issue figures compared with the issues from the mobile library that it replaced. Overall, issues in shops compared with those on the mobile libraries show a significant increase.

Contact: Dorne Fraser, Senior Librarian, Young People's Services, (01603) 222270

Norfolk Library and Information Service
West Norfolk Projects: Village Green Storytimes and Great Western Booktrail

During the summer of 1991 a series of village green storytimes were organised by the staff of King's Lynn Library. The villages selected were within a ten-mile radius of King's Lynn and each received a normal mobile visit. Over the summer holidays, ten villages were visited. The aims of the programme were to promote the library service and related activities and events to children in rural areas. Inevitably, some sites had greater success than others, but approximately 100 children attended the sessions. The success of the promotion led to investigation of ways in which a service for children in rural areas could be further developed. The Great Western Booktrail was a specially stocked mobile library which visited each of 17 villages in West and North Norfolk once a week with the intention of providing a service to children who, during the summer, would not have ready access to a regular supply of books. In a four-week period, almost 600 children were registered and visits received from over 100 adults and carers. The project was regarded as very successful, and was welcomed by adults and children alike.

Contact: Dorne Fraser, Senior Librarian, Young People's Services, (01603) 222270

Nottinghamshire County Libraries
Holiday Mobile Service

The Holiday Mobile Service for children is targeted at children in urban and rurally isolated areas of the county and aims to make books accessible to youngsters who might not have easy access to reading material during the summer holiday period. The service's two school mobiles are decorated with a theme and are stocked with a wide range of books of leisure and recreational interest. Over 50 stops are visited weekly throughout the county and, as well as being able to borrow books, children can also listen to stories and take part in activities. Though changes have clearly taken place over the years, the service has operated since 1960 and has a high profile. Approximately 7,000 books are issued each year.

Contact: Philip Marshall, Principal Libraries Officer: Client Services, (0115) 985 4201

Cynon Valley Borough Library
Readabout Bookbus

The Readabout Bookbus serves both playgroups and individual children. It visits each of 27 playgroups once every half-term, taking a box of books from which children can make their own choice, and giving storytelling sessions at the same time. Schools in eight areas are visited once a fortnight, followed by street stops from 3.30pm until 5.30pm or later depending on demand. Books are loaned to the children as individuals, using the schools as the best access point – the Bookbus is not a schools library service in any sense, but forms a part of the Library's Children's Services, and is run by a Readabout Librarian with the help of a part-time library assistant and a part-time graphic designer. The service is informal: children only need to register, and can then use the Bookbus without tickets and without fines.

The Readabout Bookbus service has expanded steadily since its inception, adding the children in three more schools to its coverage in May 1994. The total number of registered readers now stands at 3,138. In 1993/94, nearly 24,000 books were issued. Mother and baby clinics and childminders can also borrow collections from the Bookbus. All opportunities to promote the Bookbus, and the library service, are taken, and regular visits are made to school fêtes and similar events. In summer 1994, the Bookbus is going into other areas distant from libraries with a programme of impromptu activities including a clown, storytelling, and craft ideas such as face painting and badge making.

Contact: Kay Thomas, Children's Services Librarian, (01685) 885296

Leicestershire Libraries and Information Service
Bookbus

Bookbus is a special mobile library service for children between the ages of 0 and 12 which operates in selected parts of the city of Leicester. It is staffed by professional children's librarians with specialist stock knowledge and expertise in working with children and adult carers. During the day, Bookbus visits under fives groups and schools, parent and toddler groups, playschemes and carnivals, to tell stories, do puppet shows, take part in language development programmes, and other activities to promote the library service and the benefits of books and reading. In the evenings, Bookbus becomes a mobile lending library with a weekly after-school schedule, visiting some 35 street stops. It stays at each stop for about 20 minutes so that children can borrow and get help from staff about books. The objective is to take books to children on the streets where they live and to offer an easy and flexible way of using the library service which might hopefully build a bridge to their use of the main library service.

The Bookbus idea originated in the Magic Bus operated by Leicestershire Libraries as an Urban Aid holiday project in 1975. Following an enthusiastic response from teachers, head teachers, playgroup workers and others to the idea of a permanent service, the first Bookbus was launched in 1980 with 75% Inner Area Programme funding. A second vehicle was added in 1982. By 1987, the service was recognised as being sufficiently successful and important to be taken into the main funding programme. In 1993, a new vehicle was launched. Bookbus is one of the best-known and popular services provided by Leicestershire Libraries, and issued over 100,000 books in 1992.

Contact: Judith Wilkinson, Service Co-ordinator, Children's and Young People's Services, (0116) 265 7388

5.6.2 Promotion of literacy

Birmingham Library Services
Brightstart Early Literacy Project

The project was set up in January 1992 in the communities of Aston/Newtown and Nechells to explore and develop imaginative ways of working with parents to promote literacy development in very young children. The project also aimed to research into the needs of the community, from a library service provision perspective, particularly those needs of single parents and ethnic minorities. Brightstart highlights the importance of the pre-school years in the development of essential learning skills, and works to help parents recognise and meet their children's learning needs using the resources offered by the Library Service. The project aimed to encourage more parents to actively participate in their children's early learning, by running informal workshops and discussion groups. The report on the project in autumn 1993 will have significant impact on library services to pre-school children and their carers in the future.

Contact: Teresa Scragg, Children's and Youth Librarian, (0121) 235 2175

Birmingham Library Services

Beginning with Books Video

This has been produced with funding from the Government's Inner City Partnership Programme, to highlight the role of library services in supporting early literacy, to encourage parents and carers to share print all around, and to use libraries as a source of information and support. The video encourages parents to share books with very young children, and demonstrates how using print in the home can develop language and early learning skills. The soundtrack has been produced in English, Urdu and Bengali and is designed to help the libraries make links with parents who currently do not use libraries or whose access to written information about services is limited.

Contact: Teresa Scragg, Children's and Youth Librarian, (0121) 235 2175

Gloucestershire County Library

Grow with Books

During 1992/93, collections of books for parents and carers were established in all the 39 static libraries in Gloucestershire. The collections were sited in children's sections, and promoted with a leaflet and the slogan 'Grow with books'. The collections contain both books and information of help to parents and carers of children. The book collection includes books on special situations and experiences (eg, starting school, going to the doctor, bereavement and illness, etc) as well as books on the growth and development of children, and to help parents and carers select books with and for their children. The emphasis of the collections is on the 'early years' (ie, children under eight years, with particular emphasis on children under five).

Information leaflets and booklists are provided for reference in a specially designed ring clip binder, and free leaflets are available in a special leaflet dispenser.

Contact: Elizabeth Dubber, Principal Librarian, Children and Schools, (01452) 425030

5.6.3 Promotion of books and reading

Nottinghamshire Children's Book Award

Jointly organised and promoted by the County Library Service and Dillons the Bookstore, the award was established in 1989 with the aim of encouraging reading, drawing attention to the wide range of exciting children's books available, and involving children in enjoying and evaluating new books. The award is presented annually in two categories: the Acorn Award for an outstanding book written and illustrated for the 0 to 7 age group; the Oak Tree Award for the 8 to 12 age group. A shortlist of eight titles is selected in February from titles published for the first timer in the UK during the preceding year, the titles being available for loan from libraries or for purchase from Dillons. Children from 0 to 14 can vote for their favourites on voting forms available from libraries or from Dillons, and the winners are announced in July. The value of the award is that it involves children, parents, teachers, librarians and booksellers in getting together to talk about books. Over 2,000 children now vote for their favourite books.

Contact: Philip Marshall, Principal Libraries Officer: Client Services, (0115) 985 4201

Northern Children's Book Festival

A two-week festival held in November each year since 1984, is a co-operative venture by eight local authorities in north-east England. Over 40 authors, illustrators, poets and storytellers are invited to work with groups of children who have planned for the event by visiting some 130 schools and libraries. Primarily a large-scale concentrated 'Writers in Schools' programme, complemented by a number of public events, the festival culminates in a free public Gala Day for families throughout the region. The festival is one of the largest children's book festivals in the UK. Organisation involves not only a large number of visiting authors, but also hundreds of teachers, parents and librarians and thousands of children. In 1993, the Festival published *Celebrating the north east in words and pictures*, a joint project with Waterstone's Booksellers, a guide to childrens' books set in the region and a directory of local children's authors. Other publications (three books and a video) offer advice and practical help on organising the event.

Contact: Jan Clements, Manager of CYP Library Services, North Tyneside, (0191) 268 9999

Greater Manchester Children's Book Festival

A jointly organised fortnight of events held annually within the three authorities of Bolton, Rochdale and Salford with the aim of promoting reading for enjoyment and fostering the reading habit. The festival has built on its success over more than a decade, bringing children into contact with authors and illustrators. Co-operation between neighbouring authorities enables time and costs of travelling and organisation to be shared. The 1994 event, in Bolton, reached 2,384 children aged 2 to 13, involved 54 schools, with events taking place in 18 library locations.

Contact: Bolton: Mary Keane, (01204) 25372; Rochdale: Freda Fletcher, (01706) 345127 Salford: Sarah Spence, (0161) 793 3571

Young Gloucestershire Writes

This is a new project which encourages children to write for each other, and enables children in libraries to read a published newsletter of writing by other children. It has been running for one year, and is funded by Gloucestershire County Library Arts and Museums Service, supported by South West Arts. Writing workshops are held for children on a regular basis in half-term holidays. Three of these have been held during 1993/94 and more are planned for 1994/95. Children attending these free 'Bright Ideas' workshops are helped to create poems and pieces of short prose, and perform their pieces to each other. Workshops have been led by local lecturer and writer John Haynes, and local author Jamila Gavin. A selection of the children's writing is then published in newsletter form, for free distribution to children throughout the county through public libraries. Over 40 children attended workshops in the first year, with 5,000 copies of the first newsletter distributed in summer 1994.

This project follows on from the successful Gloucestershire Writes project for adults, where volumes of writing by local authors are placed in selected public libraries for the public to borrow and read.

Contact: Derek Jowett, Senior Children's Librarian, (01452) 425020

5.6.4 Support for education and liaison with schools

Havering Library Service

Local Studies Information Packs

Havering's local studies packs were started by the School Library Service some two years ago in response to a perceived need for material on the local area which was suitable for use by primary school children. The area is fairly small and compact, and it was planned to produce a pack for each of the areas covered by the ten branch libraries, starting with the southernmost. All available material on the area was read and digested and articles put onto computer so that pages could be produced to form an information pack. The standard format was some general history of the borough followed by particular areas, then by subject categories such as law and order, roads and transport, famous buildings, industries, etc. These were followed by verbatim accounts of life in the area during World War II and following periods culled through contacts made with retired residents and visits to old people's homes to tape record residents' memories. A collection of postcards and a set of nine maps made up the pack, which was housed in a ring binder with a contents page and a concluding bibliography.

Five areas have been covered in this way so far. The information packs retail at £18, and, following advertising, have been sold to primary and infant schools and all secondary schools some of which have bought packs for surrounding areas as well as their own. Within the ring binder format, it is possible for a school to expand its pack by the addition of material collected for the purpose. The project has been labour-intensive for school library staff, and is currently on hold because of a shortage of staff time.

Contact: Joan Shoush, School Librarian, Education and Young People's Library Service, (01708) 772396

Bolton Environmental Education Project

This is a service of the Schools Library Service within the Archive and Local Studies Section of Bolton Public Libraries. It carries a wide range of local interest publications including photo and resource packs for many local areas and subjects. Sets of land use maps, centred on schools, are available for every school in Bolton and aerial photographs with corresponding maps are available for many areas. Many of the materials are directly linked to the requirements of the National Curriculum.

Contact: Kevin Campbell, Archivist, (01204) 22311

Shropshire Libraries

Education Liaison Officer

Shropshire's response to the greatly increased demands for project-based information arising from introduction of GCSE was to appoint an Education Liaison Officer, initially based in the Local Studies Library and funded by the Manpower Services Commission and then the Department for Education, latterly based in the Information Service and funded jointly by the Education and Leisure Services Departments. Working in close co-operation with the schools library service, the postholder was able to relieve central departments of the direct burden of project-based enquiries coming from schools and through branch libraries, and allowed the particular needs of schools to be properly addressed. After more than three years the post was terminated because of lack of funding, although it was acknowledged to have had considerable success. However, there is now collaboration between the schools library service and the Information Service, with staff from the former using the Information Service on two days each week and charging schools (within their service agreements following the Local Management of Schools implementation) for the provision of project material copied from Information Service stock.

Contact: Elaine Moss, County Information Services Librarian, (01743) 255380

Staffordshire County Library
PALS: Pre-Admission Libraries in Schools

PALS is a library service offered by schools for their pre-admission children. It has three aims: to offer vital early literacy experience for children under five; to help with transition from home to school; and to develop partnerships with parents. It grew out of a pilot project jointly funded by the County's Education Department and the Schools Library Service which provided, in eight schools, a lending library of children's books for use by pre-admission children and their families. The aim initially was to help parents develop an understanding and confidence about their ability to help their own children develop and to become, in effect, partners with the schools in aiding their own child's learning. The pilot was set up during 1990, and monitoring and evaluation proved it to have been a considerable success.

In 1991, PALS moved into its second stage. Following meetings throughout the county for head teachers and others interested in developing PALS in their schools, over 60 schools expressed an interest in committing time and money to PALS (schools now have to buy their own books). Currently, well over half of the county's 407 primary schools are taking part, and interest continues. A booklet has been produced explaining the aims and benefits of PALS and giving guidelines for setting it up in the school.

Contact: Fiona Bailey, Senior Librarian: Children's Services, East, (01543) 262177

5.6.5 Under fives

Knowsley Leisure Services Department
KUFLINC Under Fives Project

The Knowsley Under Fives Library and Information Campaign (KUFLINC) project was set up with funding from the Urban Programme in February 1991, when an Under Fives Librarian was appointed. The project and post were made a permanent part of library provision in Knowsley from April 1993, when Urban Programme funding came to an end.

As a result of the project, an area for under fives and carers has been created in the junior section of each library, with full facilities and materials for young children, and parents' collections of books and information. Storytimes for under fives are held throughout the year; monthly toy library sessions are held in association with Save the Children; visits to the libraries for storytimes, craft and play by groups catering for under fives are organised on request. KUFLINC is also intended to reach disadvantaged children under five, and their carers, who do not use libraries. The Under Fives Librarian visits some 85 pre-school groups at least once a term, for storytimes, book sessions and other activities. Registered childminders are eligible for a special loan of up to ten items to use in their homes with children in their care, and information on what the libraries can offer them is included in training courses for new childminders. Close working relationships have been established with agencies in the early years field, and training is given in the Pre-school Playgroups Association training course.

Monitoring of KUFLINC has shown increases in membership and issues, in take-up of activities and in promotional activities, since its inception.

Contact: Jan Ashby, Under Fives Librarian, (0151) 546 2907

Hampshire County Library
Early Years Initiative

Provision for early years is a major focus within Hampshire County Council and is being spearheaded by the Education, Social Services and Libraries Departments. The library focus will involve a number of elements including user research, links with health clinics and liaison with publishers to provide joining packs for parents with young babies.

The user survey will take place in a range of libraries and more than 300 parents will be questioned. In addition, a similar number of non-users will be surveyed in clinics and elsewhere. Links with health clinics are seen as a major source for developing contacts with parents and young children. Small 'taster' collections of board and young picture books, plus library publicity, will be put into a large number of health clinics. Regular visits will also be made to the clinics to make contacts with parents, read stories to children and maintain the loan collections. The final part of this initiative involves liaison with children's publishers to provide a special joining pack for parents with young babies. A special pack will be printed and will include library and publisher publicity plus a free book.

Contact: John Dunne, Assistant County Librarian, (01962) 846084

Hampshire County Library
Family Library Link

Initiated in 1983 as the result of an Urban Aid grant, Family Library Link has been funded completely by Hampshire County Library since 1988. The service is targeted at a large housing estate north of Portsmouth and provides, by means of a specially designed mobile, a book loan and storytelling service to any groups serving under fives.

Staffing is provided by a full-time co-ordinator, whose background is in playgroups rather than libraries, plus a part-time assistant. The co-ordinator is also the driver of the vehicle. The current book fund of £6,000 a year is mainly spent on multiple copies of quality picture books in hardback plus a small selection of popular adult fiction, and non-fiction on child-related and popular topics. Current issues are 34,000 a year.

Contact: John Dunne, Assistant County Librarian, (01962) 846084

London Borough of Lambeth

Training for Pre-School Playgroups Association Courses

Librarians of the Lambeth Public Libraries and Archives Services have run training sessions for the Pre-school Playgroups Association (PPA) Foundation and further courses at Morley College for over 20 years. Initially designed to be a basic introduction to books for interested parents and carers, the sessions have recently become more structured to reflect the national recognition of the PPA qualification and the greater experience of the workers who attend.

The sessions are planned to complement and inform the other modules of the course. Course members are encouraged to discuss their own experience of books and young children. Trainers prepare standard checklists on why books are important, the range of materials available, criteria for evaluation, selection and exploitation, topics of local and national concern, mainstream and community suppliers, publishers and related organisations, and participants are encouraged to discuss these and use them in their own situations. The lists are also made available to all playgroups in the borough through the PPA's own meetings. All points are illustrated using titles from library stock including a special training collection of materials which highlight selection issues.

Courses are also provided, on request, for staff and users of Children's Play facilities, Social Services nurseries and other local groups. Each course is designed to respond to the needs and interests of the individual group.

Contact: Steph Smith, Young People's Services Librarian, (0171) 926 9327

5.6.6 Primary school children

Gloucestershire County Library

Primary School Group Librarians Project 1989/92

This project, managed in association with the County Education Department, enabled chartered librarians to be placed in a number of primary schools, to work alongside teachers to develop resource based learning and library use within the schools. Funding for the project was provided from the Education Department's 'curriculum development' fund, for which an annual bid was submitted through the Curriculum Development Teacher for Resource Based Learning.

During the first year of the project, six small schools in West Gloucestershire joined together to request the services of a librarian, who was appointed to work one day a week in each school (one day a fortnight for the smallest of the schools). The librarian spent this time working alongside teachers, helping children to develop their information skills, and helping the schools to improve their libraries and develop their use of the schools library service. In the subsequent two years, five more clusters of schools took part in the project, with a total of 28 schools being involved over the three years.

The project was forced to close in 1992, when curriculum development funds could no longer be made available from central funds. However, the schools library service now offers a similar opportunity for schools to purchase librarian time for a day a week for a year, and planned to appoint to one such post for one primary school in autumn 1994.

Contact: Elizabeth Dubber, Principal Librarian, Children and Schools, (01452) 425030

Sunderland Leisure, Libraries and Arts Section
Creative Writing Programmes

Frances Fisher RIP is a book published by Wear Books (the publishing arm of City of Sunderland Libraries and Arts) resulting from a collaborative venture between Helen East, an author well-known in the north-east region, four primary schools in Sunderland, and the Libraries and Arts Section. The author's first draft formed the basis for a series of creative writing workshops in which children from local primary schools developed and enhanced the draft, investigated the background, developed the characters, and affirmed the vernacular language. As the project advanced, children visited locations in the book, researched local legends, and involved their families in reminiscence work. Towards the end of the project, the children worked on the book's illustrations with a screenprinter, devising all the illustrations, differing typefaces, and initial letters for each chapter. For the schools involved, the project was cross-curricular involving history, local geography, language development, art and craft. For the pupils, there was a tremendous sense of achievement and creative involvement.

For the Year of the Visual Arts 1996, the Libraries and Arts Section proposes to publish a further children's book through a residency with schools in the City Challenge. This will meet an expressed need for a life of Bede accessible to primary school children, and will use a first draft as a basis for a creative writing programme. Particular attention to the visual aspects of the text will draw attention to the Year of the Visual Arts and will be produced through residencies in schools and libraries using professional artists.

Contact: Ann Scott, Senior Assistant Librarian, Children's Services, (0191) 416 6440

5.6.7 Teenagers
London Borough of Bromley
'Upfront' Teenage Libraries

Specially designed and stocked sections for teenagers (defined as ages 12 to 16 inclusive) have been incorporated as part of refurbishment of Bromley's central and three branch libraries. Named 'Upfront' from the Books for Students teenage catalogue, with permission of the company, the library is using the BfS logo and has bought its special guiding and shocking pink spine labels to create a new image for its teenage sections. That in the central library is designed like a stage set with spot lighting, and was launched with Spitting Image in July 1993. In the first month of the central library's new look, Upfront issues were 1,500 – 25% of the total borough teenage issues – and have remained at a high level ever since.

Guidelines on stock selection have been produced for the Upfront sections. The emphasis is on recreational reading with some non-fiction, and there are dumpbins and posters to promote it; GCSE revision guides only are stocked, with other textbooks remaining within their subject areas. There is an Upfront community information file, and a talk-back box with specially designed forms to collect feedback on the service. In September 1994, a special Upfront ticket was introduced for readers aged 12 to 16 inclusive which is free of fines, allows the full adult borrowing allocation of up to 12 items at a time, and charges only postal costs for reservations.

Upfront will be put into all Bromley libraries on a rolling programme. Stock is already in place, although the sections have not yet been re-presented.

Contact: Pat Jones, Youth Services Manager, (0181) 460 9955

Trafford Metropolitan District Libraries
Teenage Library at Coppice Avenue Branch Library

A separate teenage library has been established at the Coppice Avenue Branch which serves the western part of Sale, an area containing a cross-section of the district's population including both residential suburban and Manchester overspill areas. The library was created from an under-used meeting room and opened in May 1990. The aim was to encourage young people to come into the library by giving them a room of their own in which they would have relative privacy.

Stock has been specially built up, concentrating on paperbacks, and three specialist teenage magazines are taken. Non-book material was supported by the provision of a computer, a television set with video recorder and a radio cassette player, and tables are provided for homework use. The teenage library, and its special teenage membership card, were publicised by a leaflet targeted principally through schools. The membership card is aimed at young people aged from 13 to under 20, but experience has shown that the older teenagers do not use the facility much (they can join the adult library at 17 anyway) but that the main use is by the 13 to 15 age group. There is considerable enthusiasm among 12-year-olds at school and they are now able to join the teenage library in their 13th year.

The main problem with the separate library has been one of security, and advice has been taken on more sophisticated measures which are now being implemented.

Contact: Vivien Addie, Branch Librarian, Coppice Avenue Branch Library, (0161) 973 7658

Hertfordshire Libraries, Arts and Information
For Teenagers by Teenagers: Creating a Teenage Library with the Local Community

Following the destruction by fire of Croxley Green Library, it was decided to involve the local community as much as possible in the development of a new library. The plans for the new library incorporated a meeting room with external access, and this was seen as an opportunity to create a venue for teenage groups on some evenings of the week, with the library providing resources for their sessions through the use of wheeled shelving and a self issue system. Teenagers were to be involved in planning their own area including purchasing the furniture as well as the resources.

The aim was to involve a leading furniture supplier with CAD (computer-aided design) facilities to work with a group of teenagers in designing layout and choosing furniture, and a leading paperback supplier to provide a wide range of stock from which the teenagers could select the titles they wanted. They were given a budget to work within, and youth and community staff and library staff were enabled to train each other in appropriate skills. A range of benefits was perceived as accruing from the project: teenagers in the area would 'own' their library, library staff would learn to work with young people, use of the library would be maximised by its being available after normal opening hours.

The main problem in the planning stage was finding a large enough space in which to work with the young people, and this, along with the inability of the furniture supplier to provide CAD facilities, restricted the original intentions. However, working with the teenagers on stock selection proved very successful both for them and for library staff, and gave an insight into what teenagers want to read and the deficiencies of what is published for them.

The library opened on 1 September 1994, and the county is going to adopt the plan in further library developments. A team approach is regarded as essential to provide support in keeping the project going, and good links with youth and community groups assist in developing community ownership of the library.

Contact: Catherine Blanshard, Assistant Head of Service, Young People and Communication, (01707) 281582/3

Warwickshire County Library Service
'Pages': the Alternative Library

In operation now for over ten years, and re-launched in 1993 with new bookmarks and publicity material, Pages are special collections for teenagers (age range 11 to 18/19) located in all libraries throughout the county. They stock a wide range of fiction and non-fiction, much of it in paperback format, aimed primarily at entertainment and leisure interests but including material on teenage problems and areas of interest generally. They also stock quite a lot of music, principally cassettes, although sheet music introduced into one library is proving very popular. Magazines are provided, and back issues can be borrowed. The co-operation of local newsagents is sought in keeping up to date with subjects of interest to teenagers, and in the stocking of ephemera to match these. Pages have proved very popular, and 72% of teenagers in the county use the libraries.

No special facilities are attached to use of the Pages collections, and adults may use them although younger children would be discouraged and for this reason they are located as far away as possible from the children's library. Where possible, they are sited near to the music section.

A Pages Librarian in each of Warwickshire's eight areas is responsible for selection and display of material, and for promoting the service through visits to schools. The Pages Librarians meet at least four times a year, and the intention is for each meeting to incorporate some form of training element, for example a talk from a book supplier.

Contact: Wendy Leek, Head of Children's and Youth Services, (01926) 412657

5.6.8 Children with special needs
Cumbria County Library
Disadvantaged Children using a Public Library Service

An intensive nine-month project, partly funded from the Public Library Development Incentive Fund, in which staff from York School, Carlisle (a Special

Education Needs school) and Harraby Library, a joint-use public/comprehensive school library, co-operated to provide a structured learning programme to enable pupils aged 11 years, with moderate learning difficulties, to integrate successfully into a public library environment. The report, published by Cumbria County Library in 1991, makes recommendations for similar approaches elsewhere.

Published report: Title as above
Contact: Alison Chamberlain, Carlisle Library, (01228) 24166

Gloucestershire County Library
Special Needs Initiative 1993/95

During 1993/94 the Children's Team planned a special initiative for children with special needs and their parents. The initiative comprised:
- research to establish the needs of children with special needs in Gloucestershire;
- a special stock purchase to acquire material suitable for these children;
- staff training sessions to help library counter staff become more aware of the needs and requirements of children with a variety of special needs;
- a new leaflet designed to develop awareness of library services and resources for children with special needs among parents and carers;
- a touring exhibition to show the range of books suitable for children with special needs.

Research included an intensive day visiting the National Library for the Handicapped Child, visits to local special schools, and discussions with local specialist education staff. The opportunity was also taken to research ideas at the County's Share the Vision conference in autumn 1993. The stock purchase, using funding especially targeted for this purpose, was completed in December 1993, with staff training begun in spring 1994. The leaflet and exhibition were due for publication and touring in autumn 1994.

Already the increased awareness built up by the Children's Team by working in this area, has begun to produce specific results, including a lunch for one parents and carers group held in a library in the west of the county. The inclusion of a Department for Education specialist in the staff training sessions has proved particularly valuable.

Contact: Derek Jowett, Senior Children's Librarian, (01452) 425020

Hampshire County Library
Southampton Bookbus

The Bookbus began in 1976 as an initiative by Southampton City Council, when it was discovered that inner city children were not using the Central Library. It has developed as a joint project by the City and Hampshire County Council. The City pays for a driver/assistant and two summer holiday activities assistants. The County Library supplies the vehicle and pays the salaries of the Bookbus Librarian and a library assistant.

The Bookbus is a mobile library service to people living in the centre of Southampton, including ethnic minority communities. It has a timetable of street stops and visits schools, playgroups, adventure playgrounds, playschemes and other community venues. It carries children's books in English and dual languages and a smaller collection of adult books in Indic languages. It provides informal activities and story telling for children. The vehicle is purpose-built and includes facilities for film or slide shows. The outside is decorated with a colourful rainforest scene. It has a stock of 7,000 items and issues 44,000 books a year, of which 33,000 are children's books.

Contact: John Dunne, Assistant County Librarian, (01962) 846084

Gwent Libraries
Mobile Toy Library for Children with Special Needs

The Toy Library service was introduced by Gwent Social Services Department in 1981. In 1993, it was transferred to the Department for Education, to be managed by the County Libraries with its costs of £20,000 being met from the Department of Education's Special Education Needs Equipment Fund. The prime purpose of the service is to support children with special needs and their adult carers in isolated circumstances by distributing toys and helping families to cope with social, educational and recreational demands. It is provided to over 100 families throughout the county, each family receiving a visit once every three weeks enabling them to borrow up to three items.

Spin-off benefits have been that library staff have gained a better understanding of services to children with special needs, while families receiving visits are more aware of the resources of their local library, with children becoming library members and borrowing not only a range of fiction and non-fiction but also books in braille, Clearvision titles, Golden Sound story books and tactile books, and adult carers using parent collections and the full range of information services. There are regular contacts with groups such as the Under Eights Network, and with local professionals including social workers, speech therapists and advisers for partial hearing.

Contact: Ann Jones, Principal Librarian: Youth Services, (01633) 832437

5.6.9 Information technology

Gloucestershire County Library
MERLIN (formerly THEMIS): 'Kids' Corner'

MERLIN is the name given to the County Council's viewdata public information system, which is available in a variety of locations including over 25 libraries. Since 1987, the Children's Team has developed a series of pages for children on the system. The system can be accessed by a dedicated viewdata set, or by using a computer with appropriate communications software, modem, and telephone line. Children use the system in libraries and in over 50 schools. The schools library service has run courses for teachers on the use of the system for curriculum work, and school librarians regularly use it to access the County Library's catalogue of books and resources.

The children's pages, known as Kids' Corner, include book reviews and quizzes, a road safety quiz, a picture gallery, information on library events for children, and a response page for children to use to tell the library their thoughts and ideas about the system. Responses are regularly received (an interactive joke swop over one summer holiday period produced over 1,000 entries) and occasionally result in booklists or other information being supplied to the child.

Contact: Angela Frodin, Themis Support Officer, (01452) 426594

Book Wizard

This is a new multimedia children's book selection programme, combining sound and graphics with a computer database, whose object is to promote children's books and reading by creating tailor-made reading lists for children who use the programme. This is a reading and personality quiz for children aged 4 to 16 which aims to determine a child's reading and comprehension levels, and interest in and affinity to books, to inform the child of his or her colour-coded reading grade, and to produce an individualised list of recommended paperback fiction titles including colour images of the jackets; it will also provide short reviews, and encourage children to join a 'ladder of ascendancy' towards regular leisure reading.

Book Wizard is on a CD-Rom disc, updated quarterly with new titles, and costs £450 a year. Although initially aimed at publishers and booksellers as a marketing device, its potential in libraries is obvious and a library version is in production. Work is also in train on a non-fiction database which could be relevant to schools library services.

Contact: for subscriptions and/or further information, Book Wizard, 87 Broadway, Leigh-on-Sea, Essex SS9 1PF, (01702) 471166

Southwark Library Services
CD-Roms in all Libraries

All Southwark Libraries now have a CD-Rom multimedia computer. There are a number of multimedia educational CDs on offer, including encyclopedias and atlases. CD multimedia systems are a relatively new development and Southwark claims to be the first public library authority to introduce them on such a scale, allowing complete open access. A considerable amount of work has been involved, with training of staff and development of sophisticated security systems taking up the most time. A system has also had to be developed to overcome the incompatibilities that can occur in running a number of CDs on one machine. Southwark is looking to widen the variety of CDs available, particularly for primary school children.

Contact: Sue Moody, Youth and Education Librarian, (0171) 525 2830

Wolverhampton Libraries
IT Developments for Children

Wolverhampton has pursued a very positive policy of developing IT for children. In August 1993, the CD-Rom network was extended into the Central Children's Library, to give children access to *The Times*, *Guardian* and *Financial Times*. At the same time, some multimedia CD-Rom titles were purchased for the Children's Library and these are also on public access.

The objective of introducing these was to encourage children to develop their research skills in a more flexible way than books will allow. Multimedia is great fun and allows children to learn without necessarily realising it. The interactive aspect of CD-Roms means that children can navigate their own way through topics, and hopefully end up with homework that is 'customised' to themselves. Most children are used to computers for playing games and Wolverhampton's multimedia terminals show them that there is a lot more to computers than that. They also allow children who do not have access to computers at home to be introduced to them.

Contact: Carmel Reed, Principal Libraries Officer, Young People/Marketing, (01902) 312025

5.6.10 Partnerships

Nottinghamshire County Library
Youth Information Shop, Mansfield Library

The Mansfield Library Shop built on the success of the Youth and Community Service's first shop in Hockley, Nottingham (not a library site). The service opened in 1992 as an integral part of Mansfield Library, centrally located within the main library, but with its own clear identity. The addition of the Youth Information Shop complemented and enhanced the library services already being used by young people. The partnership also included the National Youth Agency (NYA) which acted as managing agent for the Home Office overseeing the initial funding for the initiative.

The shop provides print and multimedia information services to young people, specifically shaped to meet their needs. The NYA categorisation scheme is used to organise local and national information, supported by simple alphabetical indexes. The shop is designed to operate on a self-help and assisted basis. All Youth Service shop workers are trained to offer information and personal support to young people and this extends to counselling services. From the outset, young people have been encouraged to be directly involved in the development of the shop and its range of services.

In April 1994, the shop launched INFOBASE, a multimedia computerised information system developed in Nottinghamshire, using touch-screen technology to access data. Currently, the INFOBASE network is being expanded to other sites across the county.

Contact: John Clayton, Youth and Community Service, (0115) 977 4685; David Lathrope, Library Service, (0115) 977 4439

London Borough of Sutton
Up to Standard

This is a series of leaflets containing corporate statements of user entitlements from all services of the borough, aimed at different target audiences. There are leaflets covering services for the under fives, services for children and young people, and for the library services independently. For under fives, there are five statements regarding library services; for children and young people there are four statements, including one which includes provision of materials to support the National Curriculum.

Contact: Barbara Pearson, Children's Library, (0181) 770 4700

Bedfordshire County Council
Under Eights Service: 'Children First' Early Childhood Charter

'Children First', Bedfordshire County Council's early childhood charter, believed to be the first children's charter in the country, was launched in June 1994. It has 15 clauses stating children's rights and expectations.

Contact: Gay Wilkinson, Under Eights Co-ordinator, Bedfordshire County Council, (01525) 290712

5.6.11 Inter-agency development

Bookstart

Bookstart was initiated in 1992 as a co-operative project between the (then) Children's Book Foundation, Birmingham Library Services and South Birmingham Health Authority, with funding from the Unwin Charitable Trust, and is a good example of research into and development of services through an inter-agency approach. It has clearly fired the imagination of numerous librarians and others. Its aims are to promote and encourage the sharing of books with babies, to increase access to books by promoting local library services and book ownership to new parents, and to work towards the formulation of a policy for early literacy, supported by adequate funding. Children involved in Bookstart are being monitored on an ongoing basis to assess its long-term impact on them by Barrie Wade of Birmingham University. Evidence from individual libraries indicates that this project, above any other, has had some impact on service thinking, and similar projects are being initiated in other parts of the country.

Contact: Linda Saunders, Children's and Youth Librarian, (0121) 235 2175; Barrie Wade, School of Education, University of Birmingham, (0121) 414 4843

Northamptonshire Libraries and Information Service
Kids' Club Network

The Kids' Club Network (KCN) throughout Northamptonshire provides an after-school care service, and organises children's playschemes during the summer. Its services enable parents to continue working full time, or to return to full-time education. KCN is a key organisation in the inter-agency network, providing information and advice services to children and their carers. Northamptonshire Libraries and Information Service's involvement with KCN is one of mutual support. The Library service promotes KCN services and signposts carers as appropriate. At the same time, KCN refers parents and carers to libraries, often acts as a vehicle for events, and helps to ensure the success of library promotional events. It also highlights the general library services and the partnership between the two organisations raises the profile and recognistion of Northamptonshire Libraries and Information Service as a service provider.

Contact: Judith Barrett, Assistant County Librarian (Children and Young People), (01604) 20262

Northamptonshire Libraries and Information Service
Development with Early Years Liaison Groups

These groups provide a network comprising professional representatives from statutory and voluntary agencies across the county. They facilitate the sharing of information and plan joint initiatives to improve training and services for parents and carers. Northamptonshire Libraries and Information Service's involvement with the groups has resulted in a number of initiatives in co-operation with other agencies in the network, including a series of information market places in libraries and open days highlighting relevant library services, among them the Parents and Carers' Collections which have been set up in libraries across the county.

Contact: Judith Barrett, Assistant County Librarian (Children and Young People), (01604) 20262

North Tyneside Libraries

ALBSU Family Literacy Demonstration Programme: PACT (Parents and Children Together)

A notable example of a parents' and carers' programme is an ALBSU (Adult Literacy and Basic Skills Unit) national pilot scheme operating in North Tyneside. Called Parents and Children Together (PACT) it aims to develop parental literacy, understanding and basic skills alongside the language and literacy of their offspring. The lead agency is the North Tyneside Adult Basic Education Service, working closely with a wide range of local partners, including the library service. Both the Children and Young People's Library Service and the adult library service have contributed centrally to the project.

Contact: Jan Clements, Manager of CYP Library Service, (0191) 268 9999

Appendix D
School libraries: the foundations of the curriculum LISC Report, 1984

"**We believe that the majority of the recommendations of the LISC report on school libraries remain valid in broad terms**. There are a number of specific recommendations arising from that report which we would particularly urge should be re-examined by the bodies to which they were addressed and that efforts be made to ensure that they are implemented." (Section 5.4, The Role of the School Library.)

The following recommendations are numbered as they were in the 1984 report, but their wording has been updated where necessary, eg, Office of Arts and Libraries has been updated to Department of National Heritage, and some contextual elucidation has been inserted. Some re-arrangement has been effected in order to make the sequence more in accord with the sequence of the present report.

Recommendations to the Department for Education and/or the Department of National Heritage

13.2.1 To take the lead in ensuring that the role of the school library in the curriculum is re-examined. [We have suggested that this might be a joint responsibility between DFE and DNH.]

13.2.3 To take the lead in urging schools to ensure that a national initiative is taken in the field of relevant staff training for teachers and librarians, to emphasise the effective use of the school library as an integral part of the school curriculum.

13.2.5 To produce national guidelines for school library provision as advice and support for schools wishing to improve their current provision.

13.2.7 To establish one co-ordinating body for organisations in the field of libraries in schools and schools library services.

13.4.1 Together, to determine where the responsibility lies for the inspection of schools library services and then to implement those inspections.

Recommendations to Education Authorities and Library Authorities

13.3.2 To urge schools to make adequate financial provision for school libraries.

13.3.5 To urge schools to ensure that teacher librarians and librarians have adequate time to carry out their duties and to make an effective contribution to the curriculum through a suitable organisational structure within schools.

13.3.7 To urge schools to seek to employ dually qualified staff to work as school librarians and to employ Chartered Librarians as school librarians where dually qualified staff are not available.

13.3.8   To urge schools to improve the in-service training opportunities for teacher–librarians, librarians and library support staff.

Recommendations to LIS Schools, professional associations and teacher training organisations

13.6.1   To consider the establishment of modular courses in school librarianship for teachers either as part of their initial teacher training courses or as professional development **and** in teaching and curriculum development for librarians.

Recommendations to head teachers

13.7.1   To take the lead in establishing a whole school curriculum policy on information skills requirements and provision.

13.7.2   To give support to their staff who seek to make the school library effective and to ensure that they have adequate resources to achieve that effectiveness.

Recommendations to teachers and librarians

13.8.1   To be involved in all curriculum matters which concern the school library.

13.8.2   To involve colleagues in a team effort to plan the use of the library and help pupils to acquire the necessary study and information handling skills.

13.8.4   To advise the head and governing body on the resources required to provide an effective school library.

Printed in the United Kingdom for HMSO
Dd298172 2/95 C10 G3397 10170